European
American Elderly

Recent Titles in
Bibliographies and Indexes in Gerontology

Elder Neglect and Abuse: An Annotated Bibliography
Tanya F. Johnson, James G. O'Brien, and Margaret F. Hudson, compilers

Retirement: An Annotated Bibliography
John J. Miletich, compiler

Suicide and the Elderly: An Annotated Bibliography and Review
Nancy J. Osgood and John L. McIntosh, compilers

Human Longevity from Antiquity to the Modern Lab:
A Selected, Annotated Bibliography
William G. Bailey, compiler

Federal Public Policy on Aging since 1960:
An Annotated Bibliography
William E. Oriol, compiler

European
American Elderly

An Annotated Bibliography

Compiled by
David Guttmann

Bibliographies and Indexes in Gerontology, Number 6

Greenwood Press
New York • Westport, Connecticut • London

Library of Congress Cataloging-in-Publication Data

Guttmann, David.
    European American elderly.

    (Bibliographies and indexes in gerontology,
ISSN 0743-7560 ; no. 6)
    Includes indexes.
    1. European American aged—Bibliography.   I. Title.
II. Series.
Z7165.U5G92   1987   [HQ1064.U5] 016.3052'6'0973   87-17809
ISBN 0-313-25583-0 (lib. bdg. : alk. paper)

Library of Congress Catalog Card Number: 87-17809
ISBN: 0-313-25583-0
ISSN: 0743-7560

First published in 1987

Greenwood Press, Inc.
88 Post Road West, Westport, Connecticut 06881

Printed in the United States of America

The paper used in this book complies with the
Permanent Paper Standard issued by the National
Information Standards Organization (Z39.48-1984).

10 9 8 7 6 5 4 3 2 1

In Memory of My Mother

(1901-1985)

Contents

SERIES FOREWORD by Erdman B. Palmore............................. ix

PREFACE.. xi

ACKNOWLEDGMENTS.. xvii

1. BASIC KNOWLEDGE ABOUT THE EURO-AMERICAN ELDERLY

    Demographic Information................................ 1
    Nationality and Religious Groups....................... 4
    Ethnic Traditions in the Care of the Euro-American
        Elderly.. 19

2. ADJUSTMENT TO LIFE IN AMERICA

    Immigration and Settlement............................. 21
    Knowledge and Use of the English Language.............. 27
    Political Participation................................ 31

3. FACTORS IN WELL-BEING OF EURO-AMERICAN ELDERLY

    Ethnic Identity and Religion........................... 33
    Health-Physical, Psychological, and Social............. 39
    Income and Income Maintenance.......................... 42
    Employment and Volunteer Work.......................... 43
    Involvement in Social and Communal Affairs............. 46
    Intergenerational Relations............................ 52
    Family and Neighborhood Support........................ 55
    Educational, Recreational, and Artistic Activities..... 65

4. PROBLEMS, NEEDS, AND SERVICES

    Problems and Needs of Euro-American Elderly............ 67
    Services Utilization................................... 68
    Special Problems....................................... 74

5.   CURRENT RESEARCH ABOUT EURO-AMERICAN ELDERLY

        Studies of Specific Ethnic Groups...................... 84
        Comparative Studies................................... 86
        Multi-ethnic Studies.................................. 91

6.   EDUCATION AND TRAINING FOR WORKING WITH EURO-AMERICAN ELDERLY

        Theories of Ethnicity and Aging....................... 95
        Education and Training................................ 104
        Conferences... 106
        Manuals for Services Providers........................ 108

7.   BIBLIOGRAPHIES ON EURO-AMERICAN ELDERLY.................. 110

APPENDIX: RELATED JOURNALS...................................... 112

AUTHOR INDEX... 115

SUBJECT INDEX.. 119

Series Foreword
by Erdman B. Palmore

The annotated bibliographies in this series provide answers to the fundamental question, What is known? Their purpose is simple, yet profound: to provide comprehensive reviews and references for the work done in various fields of gerontology. They are based on the fact that it is no longer possible for anyone to comprehend the vast body of research and writing in even one sub-specialty without years of work.

This fact has become true only in recent years. When I was an undergraduate (Class of '52) I think no one at Duke had even heard of gerontology. Almost no one in the world was identified as a gerontologist. Now there are over 5,000 professional members of the Gerontological Society of America. When I was an undergraduate there were no courses in gerontology. Now there are thousands of courses offered by most major (and many minor) colleges and universities. When I was an undergraduate there was only one gerontological journal (the Journal of Gerontology, begun in 1945). Now there are a dozen professional journals and several dozen books in gerontology published each year.

The reasons for this dramatic growth are well known: the dramatic increase in numbers of aged, the shift from family to public responsibility for the security and care of the elderly, the recognition of aging as a "social problem," and the growth of science in general. It is less well known that this explosive growth in knowledge has developed the need for new solutions to the old problem of comprehending and "keeping up" with a field of knowledge. The old indexes and library card catalogues have become increasingly inadequate for the job. On-line computer indexes and abstracts are one solution but make no evaluative selections nor organize sources logically as is done here. These annotated bibliographies are also more widely available than on-line computer indexes.

These bibliographies will obviously be useful to researchers who need to know what research has (or has not) been done in their field. The annotations contain enough information so that the researcher usually does not have to search out the original articles. In the past, the "review of literature" has often been haphazard and was rarely comprehensive, because of the large investment of time (and money) that would be required by a truly comprehensive review. Now, using these bibliographies, researchers can be more confident that they are not missing important previous research; they can be more confident that they are not duplicating past efforts and "reinventing the wheel." It may well become standard and expected practice for researchers to consult such bibliographies, even before they start their research.

These bibliographies will also be useful reference tools for teachers, students, policy analysts, lawyers, legislators, administrators, and any intelligent person who wishes to find out what is known about a given topic in gerontology.

The Euro-American Elderly is one of the most fascinating topics within social gerontology because of the rich variety of cultures and adaptations made by these ethnic groups. As Dr. Guttmann points out in his Preface, there are thirty-five different nationality, religious, and language groups represented among the Euro-Americans. Even within these many groups there are also variations by socioeconomic status, rurality, recency of immigration, etc. that add further complexity to this rich mosaic.

As anyone familiar with this field will recognize, the "Melting Pot Theory," that all immigrants would soon become homogenized "Americans," has never been true. Our "American" culture is more like a thick stew with many distinctive "lumps" of cultures from around the world that give it such a rich and varied flavor and texture.

While the designation of this field as "Euro-American" is less than two decades old, the 310 entries in this volume demonstrate how extensive and intensive research in this field has already become. Thus, this volume will be welcomed by anyone wanting a comprehensive review of the entire field or of some part of it.

The author of this bibliography has done an outstanding job of covering all the relevant information and organizing it into easily accessible form. Not only are there 310 annotated references organized into 6 chapters and 24 sections, but there is an author index, and a comprehensive subject index with many cross-references for the items in the bibliography. Thus, one can look for relevant material in this volume in several ways: (1) look up a given subject in the subject index; (2) look up a given author in the author index; (3) turn to the chapter or section that covers the topic; or (4) look over the annotations in Chapter One for basic knowledge and overviews.

Dr. David Guttmann is an unusually qualified expert in the area of Euro-American Elderly because he has done so much research and writing in this area himself. This bibliography documents the fact that he has published more articles and chapters (11) in this area than any other author. His annotations are also concise and clear so that one can easily understand the essence of the reference and whether the original is worth pursuing.

So it is with great pleasure that we add this bibliography to our series. We believe you will find this volume to be the most useful, comprehensive, and easily accessible reference work in its field. I will appreciate any comments you care to send me.

Erdman B. Palmore
Center for the Study of Aging and Human Development
Box 3003, Duke University Medical Center
Burham, NC 27710

Preface

This annotated bibliography of published works about the Euro-American elderly is the first and the most up-to-date work on this subject. It is the longest bibliography on this segment of the aged population, encompassing 310 publications that were published in the United States during the past fifteen years. Each entry was individually selected, assessed, and examined as to its relevance for inclusion and, when found so, was summarized. The criteria used for inclusion in the bibliography consisted of two major elements in combination: 1) the work must refer to people who are 65 years old and older, and 2) the work deals with one or more group of elderly who are defined as Euro-Americans.

Euro-American elderly include both old and new immigrants, and both nationality and religious based groups. The term "Euro-American" was first cited by the United States Census Bureau in its 1971 and 1972 count of people. Taking this census as a base, more than seven million Euro-Americans elderly comprise the 65 years old and older population. This sizeable proportion of the total elderly population of the United States consists in alphabetical order of the following groups: Albanians, Armenians, Basques, Belgians, Bulgarians, Byelorussians, Carpatho-Ruthenians, Croatians, Cypriots, Czechoslovaks, Danes, Dutch, Estonians, Finns, French, Germans, Greeks, Hungarians, Italians, Jews, Latvians, Lithuanians, Luxembourgers, Maltese, Norwegians, Poles, Portugese, Romanians, Russians, Serbians, Slovenians, Spanish, Swedish, Ukrainians, and Yugoslavs. The English, Irish, Welsh, and Scots could also be added, as these ethnic groups also originated from Europe, but because English is their commonly used language they are not usually included in this designation. Not only are these ethnic groups different from each other, but they also have a differential use of their cultural and social resources, including their use of the ethnic language. The most outstanding factor in respect to these people is diversity.

Those who have misgivings about the value of "ethnic research" in gerontology are quick to point out some of the dysfunctional factors or aspects involved in ethnicity. They are afraid that such research may lead to further ethnocentrism, clannishness, and prejudice, or to a greater entrenchment within the narrow confines of each ethnic group. The social pressures for conformity may even influence gerontologists to mistrust any work that focuses on the great diversity found not only among the ethnic groups but even within them. Yet, the development of the best that cultural pluralism can offer, the incorporation of the diverse traditions into the mainstream of American society, can only enrich our culture. This bibliography was compiled with this purpose in mind.

The Structure and Divisions of this Bibliography

The issues raised by scholars, practitioners, spokesmen for the ethnic communities, and by religious leaders in national conferences and in the gerontological literature about the Euro-American elderly constitute the chapters of this bibliography.

The first chapter includes basic facts, such as demographic and statistical distribution of the Euro-American elderly. Its purpose is to provide the reader with up-to-date information about the characteristics of this population. Works dealing with nationality and religiously based groups, customs and traditions in caring for the elderly in a given ethnic group, discussions of traditional and implanted cultures, and other pertinent information are included.

Chapter Two presents the panorama of immigration and settlement of the Euro-American elderly in the United States. While their history in this country has been generally known, the fact that well over one-third of all ethnic elderly in the United States belong to one or more of the European-origin groups needs further explication. Significantly, there is insufficient information on the Euro-American elderly, especially on some of the smaller ethnic groups; more research is needed on their similarities and differences, their strengths and weaknesses, and their needs and ability to withstand the difficulties of life in this country. While the saga of the "greenhorns" has been told and retold in countless literary and artistic creations, there is a vacuum with respect to the well-being of the present generation of Euro-American elderly. One of the common misconceptions about the Euro-Americans is that they have no problems with respect to communications with the rest of society. The truth is that the Euro-American elderly are among the majority of "limited English speaking" members of the aging population in the United States. Those who arrived recently, since World War II, are often not fluent in English, and even among the oldest immigrants, those who came with their parents prior to World War I, there are still sizeable numbers who never mastered the English language. The reasons are varied. While the amount of English used in daily communications varies from one Euro-American group to another, many ethnic elderly speak with heavy accents and broken words. This fact, in turn, has serious implications regarding participation in the life of society.

The factors that safeguard the well-being of people in their old age are enumerated and presented in the third chapter. Chief among these factors are the ethnic family, the ethnic neighborhood, and the religious institutions. These are the "mediating structures" between the ethnic elderly and society. One of the main characteristics of many of the Euro-American elderly is their insistence on being self-reliant, even when their difficulties demand intervention and assistance. Traditionally, they avoid public airing of these problems and try to manage on their own as well as possible. Yet, many of them are unable to cope with the demands of modern society and suffer from a sense of abandonment. Intergenerational strife is accentuated by the mobility of the younger generation who leave elderly parents behind in old ethnic neighborhoods or in inner-city ghettos.

The needs of the Euro-American elderly, and the responses to their needs constitute Chapter Four of this bibliography. Of specific interest are studies that document the ways in which the family and the ethnic community at large are trying to alleviate the problems faced by these older people. Despite Old World traditions, despite even great sacrifices made for one's parents (who may be sick and frail and unable to care for themselves), many ethnic families lack the resources needed to assume the full responsibility in caring for an elderly dependent person. At the same time, there are small ethnic communities who cannot muster the burdens of providing services to older people in need, especially in long term care.

Identification of the needs, both concrete and subjective, and their assessment, are prerequisite for developing an informed plan of intervention on behalf of Euro-American elderly. Of equal importance is the need on the part of services providers to recognize the specific needs of Euro-American elderly. Accessibility, quality, and cost are key determinants in the use or lack of use of services by these people.

How to turn passive, dependent, and indifferent people into active participants in shaping their own future? How to involve them in the process of service development and delivery? How to maintain individuality, initiative, and a sense of wholeness, of dignity and identity in the later years of life? These are great challenges for all of us. The benefits, programs, and projects that can be used for helping Euro-American elderly to use services are the subject of Chapter Five in this bibliography. There is a small but growing number of studies in which comparisons are made between different groups of Euro-American elderly. These can be very useful for researchers who are interested in replicating such studies in different parts of the country.

Education, training, and motivation for working with elderly Euro-Americans round out the content of this bibliography in Chapter Six. Theories of aging and ethnicity, useful textbooks, professional journals, bibliographies, conference proceedings, and manuals are included in this chapter. Working with Euro-American elderly requires education and training for attaining the specific knowledge, skills, and values that are essential for meaningful intervention in the lives of these people. There are many subjects in such education that may be beneficial to a wide array of services providers, as well as to students in undergraduate and graduate programs in the helping professions. These include: awareness of cultural diversity, heritage, and belief systems among the Euro-American elderly; dealing with resistance of both the client and the worker, understanding the dynamics of the ethnic community, focusing on available strengths and resources, and incorporating both voluntary and governmental agencies into a combined force for resolving certain problems. Models that have been used in various projects and training programs are summarized and presented.

Bibliographical Resources Used in the Preparation of this Bibliography

As a first step in locating the titles that have specific bearing on the subject of Euro-American elderly, a preliminary search was undertaken in Current Literature on Aging, published by the National Council on the Aging, as far back as 1971. Books on related subjects were also canvassed. Additional sources reviewed included the U.S. Congress' Select Committee on Aging's Publication List from 1975 to present, which includes a number of publications pertaining to Euro-American elderly.

The methodology employed in securing available data about Euro-American elderly included a computer search of the aging literature at the National Institute of Health Library of Medical Sciences, and a review of all issues of Social Work Research and Abstracts between 1981-1986. These contain not only all journals in gerontology, geriatrics, social work, and all other health and helping professions, but also abstracts of works on ethnicity and anthropology. Dissertation Abstracts International was reviewed for the years 1971-1986, and yielded a rich harvest. The search of bibliographical resources encompassed the libraries of the U.S. Congress, The National Council on the Aging, the headquarters of the American Association of Retired Persons, and the library of the Catholic University of America in Washington, D.C.. A number of articles not found in any of the above resources were secured through interlibrary loans. Other commonly known retrieval and online data base sources used in gerontological research, such as Psychological Abstracts, Social Sciences Citation Index and Sociological Abstracts, were utilized as well.

Publications reviewed, summarized, and annotated follow an objective style so that readers may be able to decide on the basis of the annotation whether or not the publication referred to has the kind of material or knowledge they need. A consecutive numbering of all annotated entries is maintained to provide the reader with quick and easy access to the contents. Entries within each subject area are listed alphabetically by author. There was no intention to follow a rigid format in the annotations. Uniformity was maintained only with respect to the citation of the bibliographical data as to year, volume number, and number of pages. The publications of the various historical societies of the many ethnic groups are additional rich resources for scholars, as are the new journals in gerontology that have been published since the turn of this decade. These new journals deal with specific areas of interest and concern, and carry a relevant article from time to time.

One of the pleasant surprises in this work was the discovery of new sources to studying Euro-American elderly. Especially heartening was the finding of a relatively large number of doctoral dissertations published during the seventies. One could have hoped for a large increase in such works in the eighties as well, however, this has not happened so far. A renewed interest in ethnicity in aging still seems to have escaped the majority of social scientists. Gerontologists, doctoral students, practitioners, and researchers need to systematically study the elderly in many Euro-American groups not known at the present. The slowly growing body of published works on these people is a testimony to this observation. This compiler hopes that the materials presented in this bibliography will point out areas for further research. They were assembled here to lead the interested reader to useful sources for study.

Entries are limited to books, articles, and documents in English and published in the United States. This is a serious limitation on the number of publications on Euro-American Elderly. There are rich resources in the ethnic press, and in the general magazines of the various groups, in which stories or articles often treat the aged. However, it is beyond the means of this author to deal with them.

One of the pleasant surprises in this work was the discovery of new sources to study the Euro-American Elderly. Especially heartening was the relatively large number of doctoral dissertations published in recent years.

While the life of the Euro-American Elderly is far from being adequately and systematically studied, and while we lack knowledge about many ethnic groups, there is a growing body of published works on this subject. This bibliography is a testimony to this observation. This compiler hopes that the materials presented in the bibliography will point out areas for further research and will lead the interested reader to useful sources for study.

Acknowledgments

I wish to express my gratitude to Professor Erdman B. Palmore, Series Advisor, who approached me with the idea of compiling an annotated bibliography on the Euro-American elderly. Particular thanks are due to Mary R. Sive, editor of Social and Behavioral Sciences, at Greenwood Press, whose editorial comments and guidance were helpful to me during this project. Dr. Frederick L. Ahearn, Dean of the National Catholic School of Social Service, The Catholic University of America, who himself has experienced the joys and pains of compiling a bibliography, gave strong encouragement throughout the entire length of my work on this project. Dr. Robert L. Barker, also a professor at The Catholic University of America and Ms. Peggy O. Heller were generous with their editorial skills and comments in reviewing this work. I would like to note the help of our librarian Mrs. Anne Toohey and to thank the many librarians in Washington, D.C. whom I consulted in the process of identifying and surfacing the relevant resources. The pioneering works in ethnicity by Dr. Richard Kolm, at The Catholic University of America, and by Irvine Levine and Joseph Giordano at the American Jewish Committee's Institute on Human Relations served as inspiration to me in my fifteen years of service to the cause of the Euro-American elderly.

This bibliography could not have been written without the dedicated assistance of Mrs. Elnora McCree and Ms. Annette Newman, both on the staff of the National Catholic School of Social Service. Their patient typing, retyping, and expert arrangement of the manuscript on the computer, not to mention their patience, reliability, and good spirits, were a source of joy to me and I am indebted to them. To all those who assisted de facto, and to all who supported this effort with kind words of encouragement, a heartfelt thanks.

European
American Elderly

1
Basic Knowledge about
the Euro-American Elderly

Demographic Information

1. Gallaway, L. E., Vedder, R. K. and Shuka, V. (1974). The distribution of the immigrant population in the United States, an economic analysis. Explorations in Economic History, 11(3):213–226.

Settlement patterns of the immigrants in 1900 show that they entered the country with relatively accurate information about economic conditions in various parts of the United States. Published statistics and secondary accounts show that immigrants settled by and large in urbanized rather than sparsely populated rural areas. This settlement pattern was consistent with an optimal allocation of labor resources.

2. Huberman, S. (1984). Growing old in Jewish America: A study of Jewish aged in Los Angeles. Journal of Jewish Communal Service, 60(4):314–323.

New immigrants, the poor, the sick, the very old, and people with less than college education, tend to have the greatest need for communal supports. Ironically, many of them do not use available social services. This article presents a demographic analysis of the elderly Jewish population in Los Angeles and advances the idea of targeting services to those most at risk by both social agencies and synagogues.

3. Lee, C. F. (1986). A demographic profile of older Euro-Americans. In Hayes, C. L., Kalish, R. A. and Guttmann, D. (Eds.). European-American Elderly: A Guide for Practice. New York: Springer Publishing Company, 51–76.

First generation older Euro-American immigrants are perceived by the author as closest to their ethnic origins and numerous enough for an adequate assessment. They are currently over-represented among the age categories of old (65 to 74 years) and the old old (75 years and over.) Of the 36 million Euro-American immigrants recorded by the annual reports of the Immigration and Naturalization Service from 1820 to 1977, only about 3 million entered the United States after 1950.

Euro-American immigrants constitute two percent of the entire U. S. population, but elderly Euro-Americans constitute 6% of this population. Women outlive men, while men have higher proportions of married and lower proportions of widowed than do women. First generation Euro-American elderly receive little formal education. Women do not remain in the labor market after age 65. Data from New York City offer a detailed analysis as to use of the ethnic language, household characteristics and composition, living arrangements and economic situation of the Euro-American elderly in this city.

4.   Rosenwaike, I. (1974). Estimating Jewish population distribution in U.S. Metropolitan areas in 1970. Jewish Social Studies, 36(2):106-117.

Four Standard Metropolitan Statistical Areas were the sites for this study: Baltimore, Cleveland, St. Louis, and Washington. The purpose of the study was to identify the Jewish population and patterns of settlement. Use of the Yiddish language as mother tongue was found to be highly reliable in estimating Jewish population distribution in other cities.

5.   Smith, D. S. (1978). A community-based sample of the older population from the 1880 and the 1900 United States manuscript census. Historical Methods, 11(2):67-74.

The subject of old age needs reliable historical data. The U. S. census of the population provides such data.

Despite some methodological problems and sampling deficiencies in the census, it is still an important tool in population studies. Old age is not just a matter of reaching 65 years chronologically. It is rather a process in which several attributes such as sex, marital status, and ethnicity, constitute to a stage of life concept. Individual variations in this concept are paramount for study.

6.   United States Department of Commerce, Bureau of the Census (April, 1983). Ancestry of the Population by State: 1980, Supplementary Report. (PC80-51-10) GPO Stock No. 003-024-05236-9.

The 1980 census provides information on the population size and geographic distribution of more than 100 ancestry groups in the United States. This Census was the first to use an open-ended ancestry question based on self-identification. About 83 percent of the U. S. population reported at least one specific ancestry, while the responses of the rest varied by religious or national affiliation and by geographic area. Subjective self-reporting of ancestry may be subject to misinterpretation by the census takers and to inconsistency in recording. Nevertheless, it is a step in the right direction.

Of the more than 100 ancestry groups in the 1980 Census, 46 groups and several subgroups, such as the Basque-French, and Basque-Spanish, were included in the European ancestry groups. There are 13 European ancestry groups with more than one million persons each. Information on their concentrations and distributions throughout the four regions of the United States is presented in Tables in this report. One table lists all 46 European ancestry groups by size.

7. United States Department of Commerce, Bureau of the Census (November, 1979). Ancestry and Language in the United States: Current Population Reports. Washington, D. C.: U.S. Government Printing Office, Special Studies Series. Catalog No. C3.1861 P-23/116.

This supplement to the monthly current population survey of the Census was designed to provide users with a basic set of data on ethnicity and language. Its purpose was to serve as a bridge between the 1970 and 1980 Censuses.

Of those surveyed 132 million reported that a language other than English was spoken in their childhood homes. Groups with over one million in this category included German (5.1 million), Italian (4.1 million), Polish (2.5 million), French (2.4 million), and Yiddish (1.2 million). The supplement reveals data about elderly Euro-Americans (65 years and over) who do not speak English at all, or speak it not well. Among the language groups with 100,000 to 300,000 speakers are Danish, Dutch, Finnish, Gaelic, Hungarian, Lithuanian, Pennsylvania Dutch, Russian, Serbo-Croatian, Slovak, and Ukrainian Americans.

8. Weed, P. (1973). Components of the white ethnic movement. In Ryan, J. (Ed.). White ethnics: Their life in working-class America, Englewood Cliffs, New Jersey: Prentice-Hall, pp. 17-23.

Four indices used by this author to describe white ethnics include: 1) their numbers; 2) their geographic distribution; 3) their religion, and 4) their work status. The boundaries of this population cannot be accurately identified, nor can their numbers be verified. One estimate is that perhaps some 40 million of the nation's population are white ethnics. Americans of Eastern, Southern, and Central Europe dominate in this group.

Many white ethnics work in blue collar and lower-paid white-collar occupations. They live mainly in the older industrial cities of the midwest and northeast. They are largely Catholic, but there are large numbers of Jews among them. The four indices cited above provide a useful tool for learning about the geographic and the socio-economic status of this population.

Nationality and Religious Groups

9.   Alba, R. D. (1985). The twilight of ethnicity among Americans of European ancestry: the case of the Italians. Ethnic and Racial Studies, 8(1):134-158.

Evidence for Italian-American integration into the urban and industrial society of the United States is analyzed in this article. Many southern Italian immigrants viewed themselves as sojourners and have met with intense prejudice and discrimination from the dominant groups. Since the end of World War II the descendents of these immigrants made great efforts toward integration with other whites. Now this generation stands on the verge of an ethnic twilight for social changes conjoined with historical events contributed to the   erosion of ethnic boundaries   not only among Italian-Americans but also among other European ancestry groups.

10. Aliberti, J. M. (1980). Conceptual considerations of ethnicity: A view of educational needs, past, present, and future. In Civil Rights Issues of Euro-Americans in the United States: Opportunities and Challenges. Washington, D. C.:   U.S. Government Printing Office: 1980 Number 629-843/6080, 21-41.

The immigrant experience of many Euro-American groups serves as background to problems evidenced today, especially by ethnic women. The quick pace of Americanization in the fifties, and the changes brought in perception of self and belonging to an ethnic group by the civil rights movement in the sixties are highlighted. The focus of this statement is on the Italian-American family. This family is described as an insular, inner directed unit, traits which along with their strengths have certain disadvantages, particularly in terms of career and education. The author urges the removal of hidden and apparent economic, social and political barriers which prevent white ethnics, and especially members of the working classes, from achieving success. Jobs need to be redesigned to meet the particular educational and occupational needs of women. Older ethnic women should be given opportunities to study in neighborhood based community colleges which could meet additional needs, such as counseling and intergenerational activities. They also need support for training to increase their occupational skills.

11. Averbach, J. S. (1976). From rags to robes: the legal profession, social mobility, and the American Jewish experience. American Jewish Historical Quarterly, 65(2):249-284.

The experiences of Jewish lawyers and their struggle for recognition and success in the legal profession are reviewed from 1900 to the present. Marred by prejudice and ostracism on the part of the elite, who preferred to exclude Jews from the benches, many Jewish lawyers became not only prominent on Wall Street but attained national recognition, culminating in serving on the Supreme

Court. Jewish lawyers are prominant in the civil rights organizations, and are among the staunchest defenders of professionalism
in the practice of law in the United States.

12. Barton, H. A. (1974). Scandinavian immigrant women's encoun-
ter with America. Swedish Pioneer Historical Quarterly,25(1):37-
42.

Based on primary and secondary sources, this paper presents the
Swedish immigrants' response to the position of women in the second half of nineteenth century America. Social background, age,
and marital status were key factors in the response. Generally,
only a few upper-class women found a problem specific to women in
America. While men were impressed with the consideration shown
women, young, unmarried women quickly adopted the prevailing social conventions of gentility.

13. Baskauskas, L. An urban enclave: Lithuanian refugees in Los
Angeles. University of California, Los Angeles, 1971. Dissertation Abstracts International, 32:3752-B.

Lithuanian refugees residing in greater Los Angeles came to the
United States as a result of the Displaced Persons Act after World
War II. Many of them are elderly. They were selected according
to specific criteria to facilitate their adjustment, acceptance,
and assimilation into the larger society. Despite being demo-
graphically dispersed, and fully absorbed economically and polit-
ically in America, they maintain a sense of peoplehood based on
national origin and culture.

14. Beliajeff, A. S. (1977). The Old Believers in the United
States. Russian Review, 36(1):76-80.

Some 8000 Old Believers live in the United States, dispersed
among various states such as Oregon, Michigan, New Jersey, Alaska
and Pennsylvania. These individuals cling to the traditional
customs of the Russian Orthodox Church as it existed prior to the
ecclasiastical reforms of the 16th Century. Old Believers have
immigrated in small groups to the United.States since 1890 and
became known and respected for their self-reliant, industrious
ways.

15. Benkart, P. K. Religion, family, and community among Hungar-
ians migrating to American cities, 1880-1930. The Johns Hopkins
University, 1975. Dissertation Abstracts International, 39:3080-
A.

From 1903 until World War I, the Hungarian government supported
a program of American Action. The purpose of this program was to

gain control by financial inducements of churches, schools, and newspapers in the United States of the Hungarian-Americans, and to keep alive these people's intention to return to the homeland with their earnings. In addition, the Action program was designed to prevent American Magyar nationalists from championing the cause of Hungarian independence thereby threatening the political structure of the Austro-Hungarian Empire.

16. Bennett, L. A. Patterns of ethnic identity among Serbs, Croats, and Slovenes in Washington, D.C. Doctoral dissertation, The American University, 1976. Dissertation Abstracts International, 37:1654-A.

Approximately 3,400 first through third generation Serbs, Croats, and Slovenes live in the area studied, with Serbs constituting more than half of this population. They are dispersed over all parts of the metropolitan area, and lack a geographical locus of ethnicity.
First and second generation members are socially mobile, and more highly educated than comparable ethnic communities elsewhere in the United States. Since relatively little social pressure is exerted in the sociocultural environment in which they live for assimilation, their maintenance, or abandonment of ethnic identity are matters of choice.

17. Bodnar, J. E. (1976). Immigration and modernization: The case of Slavic peasant industrial America. Journal of Social History, 10(1):44-71.

Slovak immigrant peasants from southern Poland, the Ukraine, eastern Slovakia, Croatia, Bosnia, Slovenia, and Serbia, and the impact of modernization upon them are studied. The forging of a new working-class consciousness in the new socioeconomic milieu is seen as a result of a synthesis between old world behavioral patterns and demands of the modern, urban industrialized society.

18. Bodnar, J. E. (1976). Materialism and morality: Slavic-American immigrants and education. Journal of Ethnic Studies, 3(4):1-19.

Slavic-Americans in America saw education as necessary for trade and occupation, and as a means for preservation of the ethnic language, religion, and culture.
Slovaks especially feared the materialism and moral degeneracy associated with American secular schools. Perhaps due to this fear, there was a low attendance in public schools by Slavic immigrants. They did not embrace American ideas of upward mobility, success, and acquisitiveness and struggled against assimilation, as evidenced by writings in the Polish, Slovak and Slovenian papers during the first half of the twentieth century.

19. Cacciola, E. J. (1982).   Some aspect of working with the Italian elderly. Geriatric Psychiatry, 15(2):197-208.

The Italian-American individual presents great resistance to coming for help with family conflict or family burden. The family's honor may be at stake in acknowledging that they cannot shoulder the burden. First and second generation Italian-Americans struggle with the new cultural style, which is different from the old ways. The need for compromise may result in family conflicts. The extended family's care for the elderly was central in Southern Italian culture while the lack of it in American society brings about a sense of frustration among aging Italian-Americans as they try to care for themselves.

20. Capozzola, B. (1978).   His children's children.   Italian Americana, 4(2):203-214.

Three generations of the Derrico family are described.   They originated from Naples, Italy, and immigrated to the United States in 1904. The author shows the changing traditions, attitudes, and values of each generation as a result of assimilation and acculturation.

21. Carlsson, S. and Barton, H. A. transl. (1974).   From Mid-Sweden to the Mid-West. Swedish Pioneer Historical Quarterly, 25 (3-4):193-207.

Rural-urban patterns of immigration by Swedes between 1850-1903 are described. About 35% of the immigrants moved from Swedish to American farms. Of these, about one-third from rural Sweden to American cities, and another third from urban Sweden to urban America. The majority emigrated for economic reasons.

22. Caroli, B. B. (1976).   Italian women in America: Sources for study. Italian Americana, 2(2):242-254.

This article examines information sources, including reference work, bibliographies, and first-hand accounts for study of the immigration of Italians, primarily women, 1830-1920.

23. Caselli, R. (1973).   Making it in America - the Italian experience. Social Studies, 64(4):147-153.

The author of this article discusses contributions of immigrant Italians in both eastern and western United States; focuses on the place of Italians in California and Louisiana history, and explores the issue of assimilation versus pluralism in American culture.

24. Cerase, F. P. (1974).   Expectations and reality: A case study of return migration from the United States to Southern Italy. International Migration Review, 8(2):245-262.

Return migration to southern Italy is studied between the years 1964-1968.   Discussion is centered on the reasons cited by the emigrants for returning to Italy and about their feelings of their life experiences in America.

25. Constantakos, C. M.   The American-Greek Subculture: Processes of Continuity.   Doctoral dissertation, Columbia University, 1971.   Dissertation Abstracts International, 33:1969-A.

This is an exploratory study that stresses "hypothesis generation," rather than testing of old and recent migrants and native-born Greek-Americans of the second and third generations.   Areas of subcultural continuity explored included factors in the current setting and origin.   The former refers to ethnic language preservation, church attendances, family, kin, and communal involvement, while the latter encompasses region of origin in Greece, and urban or rural residence prior to migration.

26. Constantinou, S. T. and Harvey, M. E. (1985). Dimensional structure and intergenerational differences in ethnicity: The Greek-Americans. Sociology and Social Research, 69(2):234-254.

This study examines the basic dimensions of GreekAmerican ethnicity and its variations over three generations. Results indicated the existence of linkages with the old world, and attributes that bind together the Greek-American community in the United States. The dimensions of this ethnicity vary across the generations with the first expressing strong identification with Greece, while the second generation struggles with issues of ethnic identity. Ethnic revival is evidenced among members of the third generation.

27. Council of Jewish Federations (1973).   The Jewish aging: Facts for planning. New York Council of Jewish Federations and Welfare Funds, p. 5.

Estimates and projections of the Jewish aged within the national Jewish population are given.   A steady rise in percentages is noted for each five year cohort since 1971, bringing the proportion of aging to the total Jewish population in excess of 15% by 1991.   Persons 65 and over head 21% of Jewish households.   Federation planning must relate especially to this proportion of families since close to half of them report incomes at the poverty level.   While the majority of household heads aged 65-69 are native born, 86% of foreign born elderly are in their 80's.   The majority of Jewish elderly (87%) live alone or with their spouses. Only 7 percent of Jewish households contain three generations in sharp contrast with previous generations.

28. Driedger, L. (1977).   The Anabaptist identification ladder:
Plain urban continuity in diversity. Mennonite Quarterly Review,
51(4): 278-291.

This article discusses social change and its implications for
survival of the Plain People communities. Social change is forced
upon these people by the larger industrial - technological society.   Those who respond to the change and move to urban centers
vary in the degree of their conservatism and maintenance of religious identity. There is an "identification ladder," ranging from
the most to the least conservative, among Hutterites, Old Order
Amish, old Colony Mennonites, and Urban Mennonites. Plain People
are seen as able to maintain their distinctive image whether they
live in rural or urban societies.

29. Ellis, A. W. (1974).   The Greek community in Atlanta 1900-
1923. Georgia Historical Quarterly, 58(4):400-408.

When Greek immigrants came to the United States because of agri-
cultural problems in Greece around the turn of the century, they
settled mainly in northern cities. Some immigrants, however, came
to the south, to an existing small Greek community in Atlanta,
where they were involved in business and quickly became prosperous. They developed their own social clubs, schools, and churches
to preserve their cultural heritage. These sometimes embroiled
them in conflicts with other groups.

30. Frank, B. B.   The American Orthodox Jewish housewife: A
generational study in ethnic survival. Doctoral dissertation, The
City University of New York, 1975. Dissertation Abstracts International, 36:5579-A.

American Orthodox Jews are a subgroup of the religiously observant Jewish population in the United States. These people manage
to live in American culture by remaining firmly committed to their
traditional religious way of life without turning away from the
cultural patterns of the larger American society. Transmission of
the orthodox heritage from one generation to the next by Jewish
housewives is discussed as particularly interesting in contrast to
the majority of Americanized Jews, who, in their process of assimilation, have discarded traditional Judaism.

31. Ginsberg, Y. (1981). Jewish attitudes toward Black neighbors
in Boston and London. Ethnicity, 8(2):206-218.

Interviews with 100 elderly Jews from Boston and with 50 from
London revealed a similar attitude toward Black neighbors in racially mixed neighborhoods. While subjects distinguished between
"good" and "bad" Blacks, they were generally fearful and perceived
Blacks as aggresssive, violent, loud, lazy, and dirty. They also

tended to blame blacks for the high crime rate in the city. The
similarity of perception and attitudes is interesting considering
the fact that the London Jews had Black neighbors of much lower
socio-economic status than those in Boston. Since contact with
neighbors alone cannot explain the similarity of attitudes, other
factors such as cultural heritage may be operating.

32. Hewitt, W. P. The Czechs in Texas: A study of the immigration and the development of Czech ethnicity, 1850-1920. Doctoral
dissertation, The University of Texas at Austin, 1978. Dissertation Abstracts International, 40:6914-A, Order No. 7910974.

This history is based on an analysis of the connections between
the social, economic, and geographic origins of the immigration
and the settlement of Czech Texans. These determinants shaped the
structure and development of Czech identity and ethnicity in
Texas.   Ethnicity is interpreted as the locus of Gemeinschaft
through which the Czech immigrants expressed their response to the
environment.

33. Hostetler, J. A. (1977). Older order Amish survival. Mennonite Quarterly Review, 51(4):352-361.

Old Order Amish are described as a remarkable group of people,
who not only survive in modern society but prosper. In fact their
numbers double every 23 years. Theories of revitalization, group
protectionism, or social cohesiveness fail to explain their se-
cret, as these people violate all of them. The key to their success lies elsewhere. In the author's explanation, it is based on
preventing impersonal and bureaucratic practices to gain a foot-
hold among them. Even when change is forced on them by the larger
society, they respond with keeping the human element in mind and
managing their affairs on a human, personal level.

34. Jacoby, S. (1979). World of our mothers: Immigrant women,
immigrant daughters. Present Tense, 6(3):48-51.

Jewish women immigrants are seldom discussed in the literature
on immigration. Especially lacking are accounts of their accom-
plishments and achievements in the United States. This article
discusses Jewish women immigrants to America since the late 19th
century. The conclusion reached is that traditional sex roles of
Jewish women of total devotion to family and socialization of
children are changing. The second generation immigrant daughters
are growing up with new, more modern, attitudes toward women's sex
roles. As a result they will be more able to transcend the accom-
plishments of their mothers.

35. Johnson, C. L. (1985). Growing up and growing old in Italian-American families. New-Brunswick: Rutgers University Press, p. 245.

Qualitative and quantitative data were collected and analyzed to describe Italian-American family life in the United States. A sample of 414 individuals was obtained, in which 66 subjects were 65 years of age and over. Chapter eight of the book presents the older Italians in the study, their old-fashioned ways, and their expectations for their children and relatives. The responses of the children to these expectations are described in chapter nine. This study highlights the relatively high status of the elderly in the family. There is a pool of available relatives to share in the caregiving, and a tradition of values that places a priority on family interests over individual interests. The degree of interdependence, characterized by intimacy, need satisfaction, and group allegiance, is remarkably strong in Italian-American families, and it is a cornerstone to care for the aged. At the same time, this dependence on the family for satisfaction of needs can be detrimental for those elderly whose family ties are lost or depleted.

36. Kourvetaris, G. A. (1977).   Greek-American professionals. Balkan Studies, 18(2):285-323.

A survey of Greek American professionals and academics was undertaken. Both qualitative and quantitative type data were utilized. The former was used to assess the historical antecedents of the contemporary Greek-American professionals. The latter was used to analyze 3,549 academics, doctors and lawyers. The Greek-American professional class, which is clearly emerging, commenced before World War II. The social demographic profiles of those born in the United States and Greece are examined as well.

37. Lewin, R. G. Some new perspectives on the Jewish immigrant experience in Minneapolis: An experiment in oral history. Doctoral dissertation, University of Minnesota, 1978. Dissertation Abstracts International, 39:3778-A, Order No. 7823937.

Using 17 taped interviews with Jewish-Americans from eastern Europe, who came to the United States between 1900-1924, this study is a reexamination of stereotypes created by historians, social scientists, novelists, and film makers as to the immigrant experience. A social history of Minneapolis Jewry is attempted as well. The study emphasizes social process, individual behavior, and probable reasons for such behavior.

38. Lonaeus, G. (1973). Stand up and be counted: The Swedish stock in America and the United States Bicentennial 1976. Swedish Pioneer Historical Quarterly, 24(4):223-230.

As per the 1970 census, and for the first time in this century, the total Swedish stock is less than one million. New York City is the leading Swedish city in America.

39. Mathias, E. L. From folklore to mass culture: Dynamics of acculturation in the games of Italian-American Men. Doctoral dissertation, University of Pennsylvania, 1974. Dissertation Abstracts International, 36:455-A.

Game playing is an expressive culture among three generations of Italian-American male groups who trace their origin to the Contadino of southern Italian villages. Three traditional games such as bacce, passatella, and morra, were observed. The relationship between degree of acculturation, changes in the games, and social-interaction patterns among the players were studied. Games are viewed as precursors to future changes within the male groups of Italian-Americans.

40. McAdams, C. M. (1977). The Croatians of California and Nevada. Pacific Historian, 21(4):333-350.

Croatians came originally as gold seekers to California, but they were also fishermen, sailors, and fruitgrowers. Their immigration spanned the present and previous centuries. Today there are some 125,000 Croatians in California and in Nevada. Their contributions to these two states and to the nation are summarized in this article.

41. Metress, S. P. (1985). History of Irish-American care of the aged. Social Service Review, 59(1):18-31.

This historical review covers the sociocultural attitudes toward the care of the aged from colonial times to the passage of the Social Security Act. Irish-Americans tried to care for their own through emigrant aid societies, especially during the colonial years and until the mid 1840s. With the increasing number of immigrants, due to the great famine, the resources of the fraternal and religious societies to aid the immigrants were overwhelmed, and many had to turn to public assistance. Irish-American care of the aged during the mid nineteenth century and to the depression years of the 1930s was based on a combination of ethnic and fraternal societies, on the Catholic church, the public almshouse, and on welfare programs in the big cities. After the Social Security Act passed in 1935, private pensions and private insurance supplemented the benefits provided by Social Security which became the major source of care.

42. Mintz, J. A. (1978). The myth of the Jewish mother in three Jewish American female writers. Centennial Review, 22(3):346-353.

Jewish mothers have been the subject of many literary creations. Most of these, however, tended either to romanticize, or, worse, to stereotype them as sources of ideal mother love. Only recently, perhaps as a result of women's liberation, were Jewish mothers more realistically described. Among the shatterers of this myth and the burdens it placed on women were writers such as Tillie Olsen, Anzia Yezierska, and Susan Fromberg Schaeffer, whose works are reviewed. These women have helped to show how pernicious is the myth of endless, selfless nurturing of family and progeny. Their literary contributions to the death of the myth are, according to the author, beneficial to all women caught up in it.

43. Morawska, E. T. The maintenance of ethnicity: A case study of the Polish American community in greater Boston. Doctoral dissertation, Boston University Graduate School, 1976. Dissertation Abstracts International, 37:1816-A.

Polish-Americans in greater Boston are studied utilizing historical, ethnographic and sociological survey methods. Settlement patterns, socioeconomic position, and community life, along with occupational mobility of the settlers during the early decades of this century, are analyzed with reference to their cultural values. Further development of the Polish-American community, up to recent times, includes political activization, residential patterns, and institutional life in the community.

44. Mostwin, D. The transplanted family, a study of social adjustment of the Polish immigrant family to the United States after the Second World War. Doctoral dissertation, Columbia University, 1971. Dissertation Abstracts International, 32:5345-A.

The author examines the patterns of social adjustment of the immigrant family to its new geographical, cultural, and national environment through the responses of 2,049 Polish post World War II immigrants who received mailed questionnaires. Selective aspects of adjustment to the new country by heads of households, socialization of children, and restructuring of the ethnic identity are analyzed.

45. Munro, S. B. (1975). Basque folklore in southeastern Oregon. Oregon Historical Quarterly, 76(2):153-174.

Basque immigrants to the United States settled near the Oregon-Idaho border in the Jordon Valley. They immigrated to Oregon in the early 20th century and established themselves as sheepherders. Their new experiences provided legends, jokes, and superstitions,

centered around immigration, herding, prohibition, disease and
ethnic prejudice.   Based on   interviews and folk stories collected by the author, this article details the pains of settlement
in a new environment.

46. Redekop, C. and Hostetler, J. A. (1977).   The plain people:
An interpretation. Mennonite Quarterly Review, 51(4):266-277.

What differentiates Plain People from other minority groups in
American society is, according to the authors, their lack of interest in joining the larger society, or assimilation into the
dominant culture.   What they want is simply to be left alone to
perpetuate their own customs and society. They have faith in the
integration of small communities.   These are seen as capable for
withstanding the forces of technological changes around them.

47. Rosenwaike, I. (1986). The American Jewish elderly in transition. Journal of Jewish Communal Service, 62(4): 283-291.

Between 1970 and 1980 an increase of 3.5 percent has occured in
the proportion of the Jewish aged within the total American Jewish
population. While the latter increased very slightly in number,
the growth of the elderly during this decade was at least 29 percent. The graying of the Jewish population in America is noted
with concern. At the present Jewish elderly (65 years and over)
are estimated to be 15.5 percent of the total American Jewish population, compared with only 11.3 percent of the total U.S. population and 12.2 percent of all whites. This difference is largely
due to a low level of fertility among Jewish women. Available data
indicate that the future cohorts of Jewish aged will be very different from the present one. This difference is attributed to
being born and raised in America, to being better educated, to
more concentrated in the four largest cities in the U.S. and to a
gradual decline in the use of the Yiddish language. Greater visi-
bility of the Jewish aged will also mean greater demand for services.

48. Rudinsky, A. J. (1977). A Slovak-American perspective in a
changing society. Slovakia, 27(50):136-143.

The maintenance of Old World values and the immigrant heritage
is the subject of this article.   Incorporating ancestral roots
into contemporary Slovak-American lifestyles is important for the
retention and recognition of one's tradition.

49. Saloutos, T. (1973). Causes and patterns of Greek emigration
to the United States. Perspectives in American History, 7:381-
437.

Greek emigration to the United States was primarily a   20th-century phenomenon.   Reasons for emigration were numerous: a backward Greek economy; escape from military service; desire to make a fortune or to marry without a dowry; and escape from physical and social crises. Waves of Greek emigration to the United States occured between 1900 and 1914, immediately after World War I, and just after 1965. Each wave of emigration was a reaction to domestic conditions in Greece. Those who emigrated seldom returned.

50. Sandberg, N. C. (1974).   The changing Polish-American. Polish-American Studies, 31(1):5-14.

This article touches upon the early Polish immigrants to California concentrating especially on the   activities of Polish-Americans in Los Angeles. An attempt is made to measure the viability of ethnicity among the different generations of Polish-Americans. Differences between the first and later generations are rather striking. The greater the upward mobility and affluence the more ethnicity is diminished. While third and fourth generations of Polish-Americans are less ethnic than their ancestors, ethnicity still has an important meaning in their lives.

51. Siegel, M. K. A Jewish aging experience: A description of the role of religion in response to physical dysfunction in a sample of Jewish women 65 to 83. Doctoral dissertation, Harvard University, 1976. Dissertation Abstracts International, 38(2-A): 722.

Variation in the experience of physical aging among a group of 33 women aged 65 to 83 within a Jewish subculture was explored. The response of these women to the aging process is described as generally positive. Religion provides an avenue for compensatory values and viable female roles in advanced age for the losses experienced by physical aging. Health is a major value either as an end in itself or as a means to some other goal. Time-based terms such as "eternity" are used to reveal patterns of experience with aging and to secure a sense of identity consistent with the Jewish tradition and heritage. Yet, time is perceived also as the source of crisis, potential, and requirement.

52. Simon, A. J. (1979). Ethnicity as a cognitive model: Identity variations in a Greek immigrant community. Ethnic Groups, 2 (2):133-154.

Greek-Americans in New York City discern different types of adaptation to the question of ethnic identity versus assimilation. Two Greek Orthodox churches are the focus of this study: St. Demetrios, which has adopted modern architectural styles and dress patterns, and St. Markela, which clings to traditional and Old World ways.

53. Stachiw, M. (1976). Ukrainian religious, social and political organization in U.S.A. prior to World War II. Ukrainian Quarterly, 32(4):385-392.

Prior to World War I, an estimated 500,000 persons of Ukrainian birth came to the United States. They came as a result of U.S. industrial growth in the latter third of the nineteenth century with its great demand for laborers. The enticing offers to immigrants were matched with their interest to escape tzarist controls over their fate and their need to establish a free and independent life for themselves.

54. Stolarik, M. M. (1977). Immigration, education, and the social mobility of Slovaks, 1870-1930. In Miller, R. M. and Marzik, T. D. (Eds.). Immigrants and Religion in Urban America. Philadephia: Temple University Press: 103-116.

Slovak educational aspirations for social mobility were thwarted in the old country by the Magyar rulers who nationalized Slovak schools. When the Slovaks began emigrating to the United States, by the late 19th century, they took with them a contempt for public schools. As devout Catholics, they built parochial schools in which few students continued their education beyond learning the catechism. During 1910-1940, only 20% graduated from high school. Instead of social mobility as a measure of success, Slovaks emphasized social stability. Strong ethnic values of large families and stable neighborhood living within the confines of the ethnic culture were stressed, thereby contributing to the retention of Slovak culture in America.

55. Stolarik, M. M. Immigration and urbanization: The Slovak experience, 1870-1918. Doctoral dissertation, University of Minnesota, 1974. Dissertation Abstracts International, 35:440-A.

Slovak immigration to the United States was the culmination of population transfer from the Balkans first to southern Hungary, which began in the 18th century, and continued to the New World. Peasants in search of work left their villages in great numbers and moved west. By the end of the second decade in the twentieth century one-quarter of the Slovak nation found a new home in America. Here these unskilled laborers settled in cities, such as Cleveland in the industrial notheast, and established neighborhoods, parishes, fraternal benefit societies, and founded a vigorous press.

56. Stoltzfus, V. (1977). Reward and sanction: The adaptive continuity of Amish Life. Mennonite Quarterly Review 51(4):308-318.

What keeps Amish society together despite the opposing forces in the external world is the system of rewards and punishments. These are seen as highly effective for maintaining internal cohesion and discipline. Among the punishments meted out to deviants are simple neighborly admonishment. Excommunication is the most powerful weapon kept in bay for the most serious offenses. This, however, is seldom used or necessary. The difficulties involved in leaving Amish society, and getting to an alien world, are considered so powerful and frightening that individuals are willing to accept their society as is, along with the perceived shortcomings.

57. Strombeck, R. (1977). Success and the Swedish-American ideology. Swedish Pioneer Historical Quarterly, 28(3):182-191.

To be a self-made man at the turn of the century was both a goal and a doctrine for Swedish-Americans. Extolled in Swedish-American literature and preached by clergymen, the self-made man was the hero who succeeded from humble origins by a combination of hard work and right moral living in spite of difficulties in his path.

58. Susel, R. M. (1977). Aspects of the Slovene Community in Cleveland, Ohio. Papers in Slovene Studies, 64-72.

Most of the Slovene immigrants who came to the United States during 1880-1924, and settled in the Cleveland area, were of agrarian background. They were also, to some degree, literate in Slovene language. By the turn of the century they were able to develop and support Slovene cultural, religious, and economic organizations. These helped the immigrants to cope with the difficulties of the transition to the new environment. Assimilation to American ways of life produced a hybrid culture which was quite sAtisfying to most members of the Slovene community. The new generation, however, American born and raised, has accepted the Slovene traditions only to a limited degree.

59. Vecoli, R. J. (1978). The coming of age of Italian Americans: 1945-1974. Ethnicity, 5(2):119-147.

The first two decades of the 20th century saw the arrival of approximately two-thirds of America's Italian immigrants. Concentrating in the cities, with little education, most of them became unskilled laborers. By the 1970s the second generation under 45 had achieved a level of education approaching the national average. At the same time, "little Italies" of the working class had shown remarkable vitality. The strong emphasis on the family, at the expense of the Church, fraternal societies, and politics are discussed, along with the prospects for ethnic survival.

60. Warner, M. E. Mennonite Brethren: The maintence of continuity in a religious ethnic group. Doctoral dissertation, University of California, Berkeley, 1985. Dissertation Abstracts International, 46(09):2736-A, Order No. DA8525517.

The purpose of this study was to discover the social and cultural processes by which the group has been able to maintain its ethnic identity in the urban environment. A Mennonite Brethren community in Harrison, California, with approximately 400 members, was the site of this research. Their religious and ethnic behavior is analyzed. Each of two statuses – ascribed ethnic, and achieved religious, with the latter referring to non-ethnic convents – is described, and their far-reaching implications for the religious and social behavior of the group are demonstrated.

61. Weinberg, D. E. (1977). Ethnic identity in industrial Cleveland: The Hungarians 1900-1920. Ohio History, 86(3):171-186.

Based on interviews with 43 Hungarians who lived in the original Hungarian settlements in Cleveland, and supplemented with traditional historical resources, this study of Hungarian immigrants in Cleveland, Ohio, traces their lives in the early 20th century. Social and economic values, immediate and future goals, education, job selection, and behavior of the immigrants are discussed.

62. Wertsman, V. R. (1982). Romanian Americans: A brief overview of reference and information sources. Ethnic Forum, 2(1):23-33.

Romanian Americans presently number close to 235,000 people, spread all over the United States. They are mostly of Eastern Orthodox faith, but there are Catholics, of the Byzantine Rite, and Baptists among them. More than 95 percent are involved in industry and in professional or managerial activities. Since their appearance in the United States over two hundred years ago they made valuable contributions to the American society and have gained recognition in many fields. References pertaining to this group of Euro-Americans are cited and described briefly in such areas as immigration and settlement, experience and contribution, ethnic and religious organizations, arts and literature, and major publications.

63. Winner, I. P. (1977). Ethnicity among urban Slovene villagers in Cleveland, Ohio. Papers in Slovene Studies, 51-63.

Immigrants to Cleveland, Ohio, from a Slovene village (Zerovnica) and their social worlds are examined. Discussion centers on their links with other Slovenes in America, their relations with Slovenia, the nation of origin, and the social networks of the immigrants.

Ethnic Traditions in the Care of the Euro-American Elderly

64. Gordon, A. (1975). The Jewish view of death: Guidelines for
mourning. In Kubler-Ross, E. (Ed.). Death the Final Stage of
Growth, Englewood Cliffs, New Jersey: Prentice Hall, 44-51.

The processes set forth in Jewish law and tradition provide a
structure through which the loved ones of the dead person can
mourn his loss and become reintegrated into the community of life.
Beginning with arrangements for the funeral, continuing with the
ritual tearing of the clothes, and with the shivah, or the seven
days sitting in mourning, expressions of grief and sorrow are encouraged openly. The saying of the prayer for the dead, the Kad-
dish, is a very important element and part of the grieving process
that women and men should be allowed to participate in it. After
the burial the focus shifts to the mourner. This is the time when
the community reaches out to the mourner and begins the period of
reintegration to life. In Judaism, grief is organized throughout
a year: the first three days for deep grief, followed by seven
days of mourning, thirty days for gradual readjustment, and eleven
months for remembrance and healing.

65. Heller, Z. I. (1975). The Jewish view of death: Guidelines
for dying. In Kubler-Ross, E. (Ed.). Death the Final Stage of
Growth, Englewood Cliffs, New Jersey: Prentice Hall, 38-43.

The emergent concern with the welfare of the terminally ill is
not new to Judaism. Tradition requires that the last stage of
life be as anxiety free as possible. Death is confronted directly
with specific view of terminal illness and dying as periods when
loved ones should surround, comfort, and encourage the patient.
The rituals of Jewish custom, set down in the "Shulchan Aruch" or
the law, provide for dying in dignity. A dying person must set his
house in order, bless his family, pass on any messages or direc-
tives, and make his peace with God. How meaningful are these requirements to the dying person depends on the Jewish identity of
the individual, and on the integration of the Jewish values into
the total way of life. The prescribed procedures accompanying the
dying of the Jewish person, if followed with meaning, give an out-
let to the needs of the dying person. The dying person is asked
to repent, but the basic formula for repentance has a reassuring
quality.

66. Meier, L. (1977). Filial responsibility to the senile parent: A Jewish approach. Journal of Psychology and Judaism, 2(1):
45-53.

Are children responsible for caring when their parents are senile? Jewish traditional teaching, anchored in the Talmud and in
the work of Maimonides, is based on two concepts: kibbud, which
in Hebrew means fear, and the avoidance of disrespectful acts.
The child's responsibility is not altered when the parent behaves

abnormally. Filial obligations still hold, but Maimonides made
exceptions when the parent is mentally disturbed. In such cases
the child is exempt from kibbud as personal service (but not from
respect), while he is still responsible for arranging care for the
parent by others.

67. Smolar, L. (1985). Context and text: Realities and Jewish
perspectives on the aged. Journal of Jewish Communal Service,
62(1):1-7.

Using illustrations from the Old Testament, this article reviews
Jewish traditions and perspectives on old age. It emphasizes the
significance of care as an antidote to the elderly's fear of abandonment: how important it is that the aged stay among the younger
generations as long as possible, and the impact of intergenerational relationships on the feelings of well-being or abandonment
of the old parent. The Jewish tradition sought over the centuries
to cushion the advent of the inevitable, to support the needy, and
to urge the young to respect the old.

68. Spillman, D. M. (1985). Some practical considerations of the
Jewish dietary laws. Journal of Nutrition for the Elderly, 5(1):
47-51.

Kashrut are the dietary laws pertaining to food consumption by
religious observant Jews. These laws were followed by the Jewish
people from generation to generation since the giving of the Law
thousands of years ago. The observance of these laws by elderly
Jewish people forms a bridge with ancestors, children, the Jewish
community and God, and often are associated with a sense of peace
for the individual who has maintained this age old tradition.
Caretakers of the elderly have special obligations to respect cultural traditions and to help clients observing these laws. A
working knowledge of Kashrut is a must for dietitians who serve
observant Jews.

2
Adjustment to Life
in America

Immigration and Settlement

69. Caroli, B. B. (1972). Italian repatriation from the United States: 1900-1914. Doctoral dissertation, New York University, 1972. *Dissertation Abstracts International*, 33:689- A.

The peak of Italian repatriation from the United States occurred between 1900 and 1914, when more than 1.5 million Italians left North America. A majority of the reemigrants were male, unskilled laborers who had spent fewer than five years in the United States. Italian government officials deemphasized the magnitude of the return migration in the early years of this century because of American objections to "birds of passage." While U.S. statistics on immigration did not include figures on departing aliens before 1908, Italian reports showed that each year hundreds of thousands Italian workers left Italy to seek temporary employment in America.

70. Cinel, D. (1979). Conservative adventures: Italian migrants in Italy and San Francisco. Doctoral dissertation, Stanford University, 1979. *Dissertation Abstracts International,* 40:460-A, Order No. 800189.

This study attempts to deal with the complex record of Italian emigration and immigration. Immigrants from Italy to the United States are seen as perplexed individuals trying to adjust to conditions here by simultaneously breaking away from their past and retaining their traditions. The author concludes that despite a need to seek solutions to their poverty, Italian immigrants were reluctant to let go of the Old World traditions - even when this commitment worked against their material advancement.

71. Cohler, B. J. (1984). Europeans. In Palmore, E. B. (Ed.) *Handbook on the Aged in the United States*. Westport, Connecticut: Greenwood Press, 235-251.

Irish, Italian, and Polish American ethnic groups differing in time of immigration, extent of legacy of serfdom, and mode of

settlement in the United States, are discussed. Immigration led
to the dissolution of the traditional extended Irish farm family
and the emergence of a modified extended family form among Italians, but it did little to change the social organization of the
Polish family. While the peasant tradition represented by first-
generation immigrants is changing with increasing education and
intermarriage, there is little evidence of a change in the importance of ethnicity among both the old and the new European immigration. Service planners should be cognizant of this factor in
planning services and interventions with older persons.

72. Finifter, A. W. (1976). American emigration. Society, 13
(5):30-36.

The article discusses political and economic aspects of emigration and expatriation from the United States during 1946-1970.

73. Greenstone, J. D. (1975). Ethnicity, class, and discontent:
The case of the Polish peasant immigrants. Ethnicity, 2(1):1-9.

The author illustrates the relationship between occupational
class and ethnicity in accounting for discontent among working and
lower middle class whites which surfaced in the late 1960s. Also
reviewed are ethnic group membership and ethnic attachment as factors in the attitudes of workers toward the conditions of their
work and society.   Ethnic attachment is seen as a key variable.
Using historical data, especially Thomas' and Znanieckys' five
volume classic of the Polish peasant in Europe and America, the
author draws a comparison between Polish peasant immigrants to
America, (non-Jewish) in the 1920s and 1930s, and the Polish working and lower middle class members in terms of their political behaviors.

74. Guttmann, D. (1986). A perspective on Euro-American elderly.
In Hayes, C. L., Kalish, R. A. and Guttmann, D. (Eds.) European-
American Elderly: A Guide for Practice. New York: Springer Pub-
lishing Company, 3-15.

The situation of Euro-American elderly at present is reviewed
from a historical perspective. Attention focuses on issues of
composition and diversity, immigration and coping patterns, concerns affecting well-being, and the social networks that can be
utilized to alleviate stress. European-Americans represent the
largest minority group among the aged in American society. Until
the late 1970s they were largely ignored by policy makers, and
their needs and interests were not heard in public forums. The
1978 President's Commission on Mental Health, the 1979 U.S. Civil
Rights Commission hearings in Chicago, Illinois, and the 1981
White House Conference on Aging Mini-Conferences on Euro-American
Elderly changed their standing in public policy making and served
as prologue for their appearance on the national scene.

75. Howe, I. (1976). World of our Fathers, The Journey of the East European Jews of America and the Life They Found and Made. New York: Simon and Schuster, p. 714.

The monumental epic of Jewish immigration from Eastern Europe to America provides a well researched and a well documented description of the great transformation in the lives of millions who for several decades, starting in the 1880's, undertook a massive immigration to the United States. A work of social and cultural history, tracing the fates of immigrants in New York City, but applicable to Jews of the same background who immigrated to other major cities, it is the story of the way they lived then; the restlessness of their learning, the culture of Yiddish, and the new life they established. Of particular interest are the chapters that treat the elderly, which depict generational conflicts and the immigrant survivors, and provide valuable insights into the soul and spirit of former and present day grandfathers and grandmothers-remnants of a heroic age.

76. Jackman, J. C, (1979). Exiles in paradise: German emigres in southern California. Southern California Quarterly, 61(2):183 -205.

To escape Nazi Germany, hundreds of Jewish and non-Jewish Germans emigrated to southern California during the 1930s and early 40s. Among the refugees were such famous authors as Thomas Mann, Bertholt Brecht, and Franz Werfel, who enjoyed continuing career success. But other artists and intellectuals found it difficult to adapt to the climate and life-style of southern California. The biggest problem was adjustment to the changed conditions of life. Employment was largely provided by the motion picture industry. For those who did not succeed, the European Film Fund, organized by the celebrities among the exiles, provided aid.

77. Kalish, R. A. (1986). The significance of neighborhoods in the lives of the Euro-American elderly. In Hayes, C. L., Kalish, R. A. and Guttmann, D. (Eds.). European-American Elderly: A Guide for Practice, New York: Springer Publishing Company, 94-123.

Neighborhoods are defined as consisting of a shared geography or territory, a sense of "we-ness," and some form of formal or informal social organization. These elements function as a total system. Changes in one of these elements will most likely precipitate changes in the other elements, and the existence of all three is necessary to form a neighborhood and for its survival. Many Euro-American elderly live in their neighborhoods since their arrival to the United States and are attached to them emotionally and socially. Neighborhoods provide these people a sense of belongingness and security and support in times of need. They also provide a sense of health, both physical and mental, and consequently shape feelings and attitudes toward insiders and outsiders.

Services based in neighborhoods, or lack of them, have strong effectS on people's lives. Changes in the availability of services and in services providers, i.e. the local, familiar figures, are keenly felt by the ethnic elderly. At times people migrate to other neighborhoods when their old accustomed ways of living are disrupted by changes. Neighborhood institutions, such as fraternal societies and associations, boarding houses, the ethnic media and cultural organizations play a central role in well-being of ethnic elderly. The isolated elderly pose specific problem for ethnic leaders, while intergenerational relationships and participation in the life of the ethnic neighborhood are seen as central issues.

78. Katz, H. (1978). Worker's education or education for the worker? Social Service Review, 52(2):265-274.

Jane Addams' Hull House in Chicago was a major vehicle in the democratization and Americanization of masses of immigrants. It stressed educational programs for the working class, which included fine arts and folk handicrafts, together with studies of the humanities. Miss Addams' educational philosophy was based on the enrichment of social relations among the workers and on elevating human beings to their highest levels of existence.

79. Kessler-Harris, A. and Yans-McLaughlin, V. (1978). European immigrant groups. In Sowell, T. (Ed.). Essays and Data on American Ethnic Groups. Washington, D.C.: Urban Institute Press, 107-137.

Between 1820 and 1950, 4.5 million Irish, 5 million Italians, and 3 million Russians, mostly Jews, entered the United States. An analysis of the differences in social mobility patterns among these ethnic groups is presented, which reveals that the Irish and the Jews viewed their immigration as permanent, whereas the Italians often came to accumulate money to buy land in the old country. The Irish, who were largely unskilled laborers, arrived at a time when the United States was an agrarian economy, while the Italians and Jews, who arrived later than the Irish at the height of the industrial revolution, moved into more professional occupations. Other subjects discussed include living conditions, politics, intermarriage, family structure and community cohesion, and housing and employment.

80. Klaczynska, B. (1976). "Why women work: A comparison of various groups, Philadelphia, 1910-1930." Labor History, 17:73-87.

The author argues that a woman's decision to work results from a favorable life-long attitude toward employment. Polish and Italian groups, close to European traditions, had a large percentage on non-working wives, that is wives who did not work outside the family setting. Employment opportunities, or lack of them, were additional factors in working or not working by these women.

A model of cultural influence is presented to support the somewhat tenous correlations presented by the author. Three groups of women are identified as workers or non-workers: 1) those with a strong familial tradition and detailed duties for women in the home, who seldom participate in the workforce, 2) groups with no strong familial traditions, in which women often participate in the work force, and 3) groups with middle-class aspirations who believe that women should stay at home and engage in child care and civic activities.

81. Leonard, H. B. (1973). The immigrants' protective league of Chicago, 1908-1921. Journal of the Illinois State Historical Society, 66(3):271-284.

The Immigrants' Protective League, founded in Chicago in 1908 by Jane Addams and other social reformers, helped new immigrants in urban-industrial America. The league sought to protect the immigrants, especially those from southern and eastern Europe, who were ostracized as "racially inferior people" by the descendents of northwestern Europeans in the United States. Protection was sought particularly in employment, education, and in legal matters. The League guided the immigrants in an enlightened way, while simultaneously acquainted the public with their problems.

82. Meyer, K. C. Persistence and change in ethnic residential space: An ecological case study of the Polish in Philadelphia, Doctoral dissertation, Syracuse University, 1974. Dissertation Abstracts International, 36(10):6959-A.

This dissertation is an analysis of the residential patterns of the Polish in Philadelphia, which examines the geographical aspects of assimilation theory in relation to ethnic residential concentration and dispersal. Findings indicate that the Polish as a whole are becoming more integrated in the city. However, there are still Polish enclaves and little residential integration, especially among foreign-born Polish. Even second-generation Polish have persisted in their inner-city enclaves, despite a significant decline in their overall residential segregation.

83. Prager, E. H. (1986). Elderly movers to Israel. Journal of Cross-Cultural Gerontology, 1(1):91-102.

A sample of 223 English-speaking relocators to Israel was surveyed at a one-day conference dealing with life in Israel. Investigation of the relationship between types of activity participation, and post-relocation adjustment and morale was the focus of this effort. Only involvement in formal activities, such as ac-

tive participation in organizations, philanthropic voluntary activities, and/or civic and political movements, were found to be
significantly correlated with an index of adjustment. Participation in informal, high intimacy, or solitary activities was found
to have no significant effect on indicators of adjustment/morale.
Long distance relocation necessitates the forging of new relationships between the self and the environment. Formal, task-
-centered areas of activity constitute sources of involvement and
provide an arena in which continuity between present and past concepts of self may be facilitated.

84. Seifer, N. (1973). Absent from the majority: Working-class
women in America. New York: The American Jewish Committee.

According to the author far less is known about working-class
women than about either middle-class or poorer women. This article describes the reactions of white ethnic women and their families to changes that treaten their life-style, and cites statistics to indicate their unique situation regarding work, family,
education, and community expectations. Working-class women, the
author says, can, and probably will, provide a strong, humanizing
influence in political life, the labor movement, and in their
communities, as they find advocates, gain skills to organize, and
speak out on issues that affect not only their own lives but those
of many others. A set of recommendations conclude this study.

85. Torgoff, S. T. (1983).   Immigrant women, the family, and
work: 1850-1950. In Rosof, P. J. F., Zeisel, W., Quandt, J. B.
and Maayan, M. (Eds.). Ethnic and Immigration Groups: The United
States, Canada, and England, New York: The Havorth Press, pp.
31-47.

This article reviews studies published during the 1970s which
deal with a little explored subject: immigrant women mainly in
European ethnic groups. Recent interest in both immigration history and women's history make this area of investigation a relevant one for the study of European-American elderly. Much of the
data reviewed refer to the experiences of a generation who are the
present elders. Studies cited provide an interesting picture of
immigrant women's coping capacities with adverse conditions, both
inside and outside of the family settings. The economic and social roles they played, along with their organizing activities in
forming labor unions are highlighted. The notion that immigrant
women were passive victims of their sex and ethnicity is refuted.

86. Ueda, R. (1980). Naturalization and citizenship. In S. T.
Thernstrom, A. Orlov, and O. Handlin (Eds.). Harvard Encyclopedia
of American Ethnic Groups. Cambridge, MA: Belknap Press of Harvard University Press, 734-748.

This article presents the tortous history of naturalization and
citizenship from the colonial times to the present—which affected

and still affect Euro-American and other people and their lives in America. The complicated legal standards and administrative procedures employed since the first immigrants arrived to the new land are traced in a historical context encompassing the colonical period, in which the origins of citizenship in the United States were established, through the New Republic, and subsequent development of this country into its leading position among the nations. Along the way millions of immigrants had to experience often contradicting rules and relations affecting their legal and political status, their fortunes and welfare. Definitions of "aliens" waxed and vaned with each period, largely on the basis of economical considerations of the growing country, but the story and the history are full of prejudices, fears, hopes and expectations of both rulers and subjects.

The Bureau of Naturalization was formed in 1913 mainly to deal with the concern over the "critical differences" between the old immigrants of northern and western Europe, who came to secure religious and political freedom, and between the new immigrants of eastern and southern Europe, who came "only for material betterment." Efforts to educate the newcomers in the American democratic ways of life are well documented, and the roles of civic and religious organizations to promote Americanization are described. By the mid 20th century the racial restrictions on naturalization, and many of the prejudices against various ethnic groups, were replaced by a growing recognition that all ethnic groups had the capacity to assimilate into the national civic culture, and U.S. citizenship was opened to all. The development of American citizenship has been a vital ingredient in forming an American nation out of the multiplicity of ethnic groups.

87. Prager, E. (1985). Older English-speaking immigrants in Israel: Observations on their perceived adjustment. Journal of Jewish Communal Service, 61(3):209-218.

The voluntary relocation of the aged to another country has received scant attention by gerontologists, especially the immigration to Israel by English speaking elderly Jews from the U.S., Canada, Great Britain, Australia, and South Africa. This article reports on, and discusses, the meaning of data collected from 223 older English-speaking relocators to Israel. The majority of these relocated because of ideological reasons, not out of family considerations. Many were active in Jewish organizational life in their countries of origin, especially in America. While the majority of these immigrants felt rather integrated into Israeli society, and have found a "niche" or corner to live more or less comfortably, many need assistance, especially counseling to cope with the hardships of the transition to a new culture.

Knowledge and Use of the English Language

88. Berman, R. U., Weiner, A. S. and Fishman, G. S. (1986). Yiddish: It's more than a language; in-service training for staff of a Jewish home for the aged. Journal of Jewish Communal Service, 62(4):328-334.

The present generation of Ashkenazic Jewish elderly has a special relationship to the Yiddish language. Yiddish is the key to their culture and lifestyle - the very heart of their existence. This is true particularly for Orthodox Jews who comprise almost the entire population of an Orthodox Jewish Home for the aged. The majority of these residents learned Yiddish as their primary language, and its use in their daily lives is taken for granted by the administrators in all activities. While Yiddish is used by the residents of the Home, the great majority of the staff is of different ethnic, racial and cultural backgrounds. Problems in communication and mutual understanding are mainly attributed to the language barrier. As the pool of Yiddish speaking health care professionals is seriously limited, alternative approaches are necessary. One of the alternatives used with growing success at the Home entails the teaching of the staff to become familiar with the world of Yiddish. Special training sessions developed by the management include the use of training materials to expand the staff's knowledge of Yiddish; discussion and use of a language lab, and audio-visual methods. Participants in the training sessions indicate an improved understanding of the residents. Speaking in Yiddish by the staff, however limited their vocabulary, is a source of joy for the aged.

89. Fishman, J. A. (1980). Language maintenance. In S. T. Thernstrom, A. Orlov, and O. Handlin (Eds.). Harvard Encyclopedia of American Ethnic Groups. Cambridge, MA: Belknap Press of Harvard University Press, 629-638.

The maintenance of an ethnic language, as an expression of ethnicity and culture other than the dominant English in the United States, is a complex phenomenon. Data collected by the U.S. Census Bureau do not provide accurate estimates with respect to actual use of the mother tongue by ethnic people. Nor do these data specify whether they refer to active or passive use; whether speaking or literacy is being measured, or whether the content studied refers to listening or understanding a foreign language.
    Language shifts in general can take three distinct forms: 1) from immigrant native tongue to the language of the host society; 2) shift of indigenous language in favor of intrusive language, which is usually accomplished through conquest or other severe dislocation of the original population; and 3) disruption of former diglossia through the reversal of intracommunal class, status, and power position. A degree of societal bilingualism continues in the same settings in which linguistic shifts of one kind or another has occurred. Despite the predominance of the English language, some eight million inhabitants claimed in 1975 the primary use of some language other than English, while another 17 million used both English and another language in their daily life.
    The difficulties involved in maintenance of a foreign language at either the informal, spontaneous level spoken in the family and ethnic neighborhood, or at the more formal, written level are discussed, with a pessimistic outlook for long range maintenance of the ethnic languages and ethnic heritages in the United States.

90. Hunter, C. and Harman, D. D. (1979). <u>Adult illiteracy in the United States, A report to the Ford Foundation.</u> New York: McGraw Hill.

What is adult illiteracy? Who are the adult illiterates? What is being done about adult illiteracy? What should be done, by whom, and how? These are the central questions raised, and answered, in this report. Conventional literacy refers to the ability to read, write and comprehend texts on familiar subjects, and to understand the signs, labels, instructions, and directions that are necessary to get along within one's environment. Functional literacy means the possession of skills deemed as necessary by particular persons and groups to fulfill self-determined objectives in social and community settings. Adult illiteracy is the term used by the researchers for those individuals who do not possess the above abilities and skills. Available statistics do not provide accurate figures about the number of adult illiterates as there are no commonly accepted standards for the definition of adult illiteracy. It is known, however, that both ethnic minorities and the old (65 years and over) comprise the most educationally disadvantaged groups. They also suffer, perhaps as a consequence, from other major social and economic disadvantages.

Only a small proportion of those suffering from functional illiteracy enter educational programs designed to provide them with the tools needed for survival in a literate society. Establishment of new, pluralistic, community-based initiatives to serve the disadvantaged identified above is the number one recommendation for action by policymakers.

91. Knox, A. B. (1977). <u>Adult development and learning.</u> San Francisco, California: Jossey-Bass.

Findings from over one thousand studies of adult development and learning needs are synthesized in this book. The author describes the circumstances under which adults learn most effectively, the ways in which learning ability is affected by age, by family roles, social activities, occupation, personality characteristics, and health. The studies reviewed reflect, almost exclusively, the experience of white middle-class Americans.

92. Landfors, A. and Hasselmo, N. (1976). On the Swedish-American language. <u>Swedish Pioneer Historical Quarterly</u>, 25(1):3-12.

American Swedish is a mixed language. It is shaped by the influence of English and is bound by linguistic laws. Malm and Anna Olsson have documented it in their books, citing its importance in the study of cultural history.

93. Nur, F. Language maintenance efforts of several ethnic groups in Allegheny County, Pennsylvania. Doctoral dissertation, University of Pittsburg, 1978. Dissertation Abstracts International, 40: 829-A, Order No. 7917489.

This is a study of language maintenance efforts (with 40 national parish pastors and 13 leaders of ethnic fraternal and cultural organizations) and on its use in various activities and services. Eight ethnic groups in Allegheny County, Pennsylvania, were included in the study. Examination of the relationship between language maintenace efforts and organizational features encompassed such variables as size, homogeneity, percentage of foreign-born membership, and attitudes of the leaders toward the ethnic language and its future prospects.

94. Simowski, M. J. (1983). Language problems as a barrier to service delivery among elderly of Eastern European descent. Washington, D.C.: National Council on the Aging Conference, March 15, 1983.

A survey instrument in four languages: English, Polish, Slovak, and Ukrainian, was administered to 1,380 Wayne County senior citizens of Eastern European descent. The purpose of the survey was to develop a needs profile and to ascertain the extent of difficulty in understanding English. Poor education and English language deficiencies were cited as major causes of services under-utilization among these ethnic senior citizens. Difficulties in understanding the doctor, reading labels on medications, and filling out government forms are listed as problems that need to be addressed by Area Agencies on Aging with similar ethnic composition of their aged population.

95. Virtanen, R. (1979). The Finnish language in America. Scandinavian Studies, 51(2):146-161.

New awareness of the treasures contained in preserving languages spoken by immigrants to America, especially Finnish, who are discussed by the author, a second-generation Finnish-American, relates the dispersion pattern of Finnish immigrants and compares English and Finnish phonology.

96. Wiley, T. G. (1986). The significance of language and cultural barriers for the Euro-American elderly. In Hayes, C. L., Kalish, R. A. and Guttmann, D. (Eds.). European-American Elderly: A Guide for Practice. New York: Springer Publishing Company, 35-50.

Many Euro-American elderly fail to become proficient in English despite their long stay in this country. Among the reasons cited for this phenomenon are the negative attitudes of the English speaking majority toward ethnic people, and the insistence of many elderly people on preserving the ethnic language as a sign of loyalty to one's culture. Ethnic languages provide these persons with a sense of personal identity and signify group membership as well. The age factor in learning a second language in adulthood cannot be ignored. In general, the older a person, the more difficult for him or her to acquire a second language. Service providers are urged to consider various options open to ethnic elderly who are deficient in the English language to assure greater participation in programs and benefits for the elderly.

Political Participation

97. Bechill, W. (1979). Politics of aging and ethnicity. In D. E. Gelfand & A. J. Kutzik (Eds.). Ethnicity and aging. New York: Springer, 137-148.

Analyzing the policy of the Administration on Aging toward ethnicity, the author shows that differences among the aged with respect to their ethnic backgrounds were ignored until the 1971 White House Conference on Aging. Since that time priority for minorities aimed projects were supported, while the needs of white ethnics, i.e., Euro-Americans, were largely ignored. A more enlightened social policy in aging is needed to strengthen ethnic organizations and the informal helping networks, including those of the white ethnics. The Administration on Aging should be regarded by all ethnics as a support system for old people in the United States, a system involved in planning, advocating and providing services for all aged. Diversity of the older population should always be respected in program planning and administration and in service delivery. Access to and availability of services offered under various public laws to the ethnic elderly, and involvement of the local ethnic community in program formulation and development are advocated.

98. Gerson, L. L. (1976). Ethnics in American politics. Journal of Politics, 38(3):336-346.

Ethnics, or hyphenated Americans, are seen as more interested in achieving dignity, equality, respectability and access to American benefits and values them in winning political power, championing the causes of the old country, or exalting culture and religion. There is a need to gain more knowledge about the preferences and political behaviors of the ethnics. The role of ethnicity in American politics and in conducting foreign diplomacy needs further research as well.

99. McCourt, K. Women and grass-roots politics: A case study of working-class women's participation in assertive community organizations. Doctoral dissertation, University of Chicago, 1975. Dissertation Abstracts International, 36:2440-A.

In the late 1960s and early 1970s urban community groups de-
manded greater integration in housing and schools.

The role of white ethnic working class women in assertive community organization and political behavior is discussed. The
research was carried out on the Southwest side of Chicago, in
which a number of grass-roots organizations were formed in those
years, and where women were active especially in providing leadership and organization.

100. Novak, M. (1973). Probing the new ethnicity. In Ryan, J.
(Ed.). White Ethnics: Their Life in Working Class America.
Englewood Cliffs, New Jersey: Prentice-Hall, 158-167.

Several theses about white ethnics that are conventional but
wrong lead the discussion of the new ethnicity by Novak. Among
these are the following: that ethnic consciousness is regressive;
that it is for the old; that it is divisive and breeds hostility
among the various ethnic groups; that it will disappear; that it
is all right for the minorities, but not for the mainstream, and
that an emphasis on the white ethnics will detract from the priority for other, more disadvantaged, groups in society.

Three components of the new ethnicity warrant serious consideration: one is the reawakened interest in cultural pluralism, the
other, the personal need for making a conscious effort to learn
about one's own ethnic roots, and the third, a need to share in
the struggle for greater harmony and justice for all members of
society. Such a vision of the new ethnicity gives hope to a
better tomorrow.

101. Pavlak, T. J. Ethnic identification and political behavior.
Doctoral dissertation, University of Illinois at Urbana-Champaign,
1971. Dissertation Abstracts International, 32:5860-A.

The author studies the nature of ethnic identification by testing two theories, and the effect of ethnicity on political behavior, including party affiliation and voting preference, political
alienation, and racial antagonism. Data were obtained from interviews with a sample of 354 respondents of Irish, Polish, Lithuanian, Slovak and Mexican backgrounds in an ethnic community in
Chicago. A measure of ethnic identification, developed by the
author, is presented.

3
Factors in Well-Being
of Euro-American Elderly

Ethnic Identity and Religion

102. Abramson, H. J. (1975). The religioethnic factor and the
American experience: Another look at the three generations hypothesis, Ethnicity, 2(2):163-177.

This article presents a theoretical and empirical examination of
the religious behavior of different American ethnic groups with
controls for social generation in the United States. The principle of "third generation interest" in ethnicity, and the "rise-
decline - and-rise" of religious association are not supported by
data. Ethnic variation in religious behavior over generational
time is more frequently the case, depending largely on the religioethnic culture itself. Grandchildren of immigrants experience
their "third generation" under vastly different conditions than
their grandfathers. Religious behavior is affected more by the
traditions and styles of ethnic life and the local community than
by the external pressures of the larger society.

103. Collier, C. M. (1979). A community study of aging and
religion among rural Pennsylvania Germans. Doctoral dissertation,
University of Massachusetts, 1978. Dissertation Abstracts International, 39(8-A):5012, Order No. 7901986.

A predominantly rural German Protestant group of elderly people
in southeastern Pennsylvia was studied. Subjects were 63 men and
101 women aged 65 and over. A number of research tools were
utilized, including participant observation and key informant
interviews. Two main findings indicate that religion was the
major factor in the interaction of these people with each other
and their community, and that they were all vital, integrated and
participating members of their churches.

104. Guttmann, D. (1974). Social indicators, Jewish identity and
morale of the aged. Doctoral dissertation, The Catholic University of America, 1974. Dissertation Abstracts International,
35(9):6236-6237 (Studies in Social Work No. 101).

Improving the quality of life for the aged has been the implicit aim of both the human and the social services available to our aged citizens. Implicit in this aim is the need to explore the factors which have a direct bearing on older people to live meaningful and psychologically healthy lives. A correlational design was utilized with a sample of 162 subjects, drawn by stratified random sampling procedures from two settings, to study the effects of differential exposure of Jewish aged to their social and cultural environments.

Married aged in both settings exhibited higher morale than the widowed, divorced, separated or never married single aged. American born and raised older adults had higher morale than their peers from East European countries. Health and Jewish identity were significantly associated with morale in both groups, while social conditions and the quality of social interaction were additional influential predictors of morale. Implications of these findings for programming of services and for future research are delineated.

105. Johnson, C. J. (1982). An oral history study of the religiosity of fifty Chech-American elderly. Doctoral dissertation, Iowa State University, 1981. **Dissertation Abstracts International,** 42(11):4945A, Order No. DA8209133.

An oral history approach was employed to describe and analyze the religiosity of fifty Chech-American elderly in Iowa. The dissertation argues for the usefulness of oral history research in the study of religiosity in old age. Current assessment of religiosity research and description and interpretation of the religiosity and the heritage of these senior citizens are elaborated.

106. Johnson, C. J. and Hraba, J. (1984). Life histories and research on religiosity among Czech-American elderly in the Midwest: The evolution of ecumenism and humanism. **Journal of Religion and Aging,** 1(1):71-83.

In-depth life histories to describe the subjective lives and religiosity of fifty Czech-American elderly in Iowa were obtained in a mixture of religious and secular questions. This method is assumed to tap effectively the concerns of the subjects, as it is considered to be a non-threatening way for obtaining data. Results indicate ecumenism and humanism among these elderly, which coincides with their liberal religious heritage. Findings also suggest that rural Czech-American elderly, who are either exclusively mainline church-goers of freethinkers, find ultimate meaning in life through ecumenism and humanism rather than through sectarianism.

107. Kalish, R. A. and Creedon, M. A. (1986). Religion and the church. In Hayes, C. L., Kalish, R. A. and Guttmann, D. (Eds.). European American Elderly: A Guide for Practice. NEW YORK: SPRINGER PUBLISHING COMPANY, 124-142.

The importance of religion in the lives of Euro-American elderly is presented. Examination centers on faith, including values and practices, on the churches and their programs, and on the clergy and other people who represent the church, the denomination, or the congregation. Many Euro-Americans came to this country to escape religious persecution and prejudice in the old country. Historical records provide evidence to the critical roles religious institutions played in the settlement of the immigrants. Churches were often the center of life for the entire community. Even today the ethnic church occupies an important place in the lives of many Euro-American elderly. However, ethnic groups are not homogeneous with respect to religious affiliation. Some ethnic groups, such as the Greeks, are composed of one denomination, others have more than one denomination. These may be seen as separate ethnic groups.

Religious faith encompasses feelings, experiences and knowledge, and are expressed in actual behavior as a result of the above elements. The great majority of Euro-American elderly value their religions, but the groups within the population vary greatly with respect to religious practices. Ethnic ties are generally indicative of religious affiliation, yet there are many ethnic people with strong community ties who do not attend church. Clergy serve as counselors, organizers, advocates, and educators. Ministry to the elderly is seen as a major role. Problems faced by ethnic churches include diminishing membership, aging of the congregants and of the clergy, and delegation of tasks to an increasing number of deacons and laity.

108. Kalish, R. A. (1986). The meanings of ethnicity. In Hayes, C. L., Kalish, R. A. and Guttmann, D. (Eds.). European-American Elderly: A Guide for Practice. New York: Springer Publishing company, 16-34.

Ethnicity has many meanings for the individual and for the ethnic group. Not all the variables used to define ethnicity are equal in their importance for individual or even group well-being. Differences in age cohort and immigration cohort membership entail differences in life experiences and in attitudes toward personal, national, and world events by ethnic individuals.

A person's sense of connectedness and belonging to an ethnic group are influenced by many factors, and these determine the extent and the degree of assimilation into the larger society. Membership in a Euro-American ethnic community and its meaning are discussed, and shared values, ethnic pride, and loyalty, along with linkage to one's roots, are highlighted.

109. Linkh, R. M. Catholicism and the European immigrant, 1900–1924: A chapter in American social thought. Doctoral dissertation, Columbia University, 1973. Dissertation Abstracts International, 34: 3934-A.

Church leaders during the height of the mass immigration from eastern, southern, and central Europe rejected the idea of hasty "Americanization" of the immigrants. They opted instead for gradual assimilation and for the preservation of the newcomers' language and culture, thus paving the way for the emergence of cultural pluralism. The reluctance to encourage rapid transformation of the immigrants to "Americans" was mainly based on fear that such efforts may mean the loss of the immigrants to the Catholic Church.

110. Lopreato, J. (1973). Religion and the immigrant experience. In Ryan, J. (Ed.). White Ethnics: Their Life in Working Class America. Englewood Cliffs, New Jersey: Prentice Hall, 59–64.

Next to the family, the Catholic religion has been the most critical institution for the Italian immigrants to America. The religious life of the people in southern Italy has never been pious. Attendance at churches, with the exception of major holidays, was usually limited to few older widows, spinsters and bachelors. The relationship to the priest was hampered first by the perception that he represents the ruling classes, and especially the landowners, then to fear, and finally to very different ideas and customs related to the expression of religiosity, practices that were rejected by the priests in general.

When the peasants came to America they found a church organization and culture that was alien to their experience. The churches were dominated by the Irish. In the ensuing struggle for dominance and self-expression, conflicts between the generations of the "oldtimers" and the "newly educated" grew rapidly. These conflicts and problems disappeared in the late 30s and 40s, when the Italians were finally assimilated into the American society. Today there is a general recognition among Italian-Americans of the Catholic churches' importance in the lives of their constituents, yet trends of secularism and skepticism toward church authority still linger.

111. Mostwin, D. (1972). "In search of ethnic identity," Social Casework, 53(5):307–316.

A glimpse into "the safe privacy of a common mental construction" of a group of 2,049 uprooted persons from Poland, immigrants to the United States after World War II, is offered. Changes within the ethnic identity and related factors are summarized. Perceptions of self, and others' perception in regard to subjects' ethnic identity are presented. The majority of the respondents considered themselves primarily Polish and believed that their fellow Americans looked upon them as Polish. Sensitivity to cultural differences, interest in a client's ethnic background, and understanding its meaning to him/her are important factors in therapy with Euro-American clients.

112. Nelson, H. M. and Allen, H. D. (1974). Ethnicity, American-ization, and religious attendance. American Journal of Sociology, 79(4):906-922.

Inter-ethnic variations in patterns of Americanization, as evi-denced by religious attendance, were studied using secondary ana-lysis of data on New York City Catholics. The respondents were grouped into western, eastern, and southern European categories based on country of origin. First generation Catholics' religious attendance showed no meaningful differences, while there were sub-stantial differences among the second generation respondents. Western Europeans showed an increase in attendance. These find-ings illustrate the importance of inter-ethnic variations in pat-terns of Americanization.

113. Novak, M. (1973). Confessions of a white ethnic. In Ryan, J. (Ed.). White Ethnics: Their Life in Working-Class America, Englewood Cliffs, New Jersey: Prentice Hall, 24-36.

In this richly illustrated, highly emotional article, the author recounts his early stirrings of ethnic consciousness. This feel-ing later blossomed into a full-blown, self appointed leadership in white ethnic America. Insights gained during the long process of awakening to what it means to be a Slovak-American were put to use to explain important aspects and expressions of white ethnic identity. Particularly relevant for the study of Euro-American elderly is the author's description of the consequences of inter-action between white ethnics and the dominant groups in society.

Transition into an accepted status, by way of success in Amer-ica, has its own price. Often this price is the rejection of one's own roots, and subsequent feelings of emptiness and isola-tion. Ethnic values of high family connectedness, group responsi-bility, and communal life, are juxtaposed with the loneliness often felt by the outwardly successful members of the majority culture.

114. Pinsker, S. (1975). Piety as community: The Hasidic view, Social Research, 42(2):230-246.

The life, philosophy, and attitudes of Hasidic Jews in the United States is discussed, speculating on whether the traditional Jewish community is currently disintegrating.

115. Roche, J. P. (1984). Social factors affecting cultural, national and religous ethnicity: A study of suburban Italian-Americans. Ethnic Groups, 6(1):27-45.

This study examined the distribution of attitudes to ethnicity by sex, generation, income, suburb, age, education and ethnic identity among Italian-Americans and other ethnics in two suburbs of Providence, Rhode Island. A total of 248 respondents completed a schedule consisting of sixty questions and thirty ethnic statements.
Ethnicity was found to be positively associated with age: weaker levels of ethnicity were found among the young; stronger levels among the old. Ethnic identification as "Italian," as opposed to "American of Italian descent," "American" or "other" is an indicator of a person's sense of closeness to, or distance from others, of the same ethnic background. The degree of attachment to the cultural, rational, and religious aspects of ethnicity is seen as decline among middle and upper class Italians. Religious ethnic traditions were on the wane, while cultural aspects of ethnicity received most support.

116. Shanabruch, C. H. The Catholic Church's Role in the Americanization of Chicago's immigrants: 1833-1928. Doctoral dissertation, University of Chicago, 1975. Dissertation Abstracts International, 36:4718-A.

The Catholic Church's role in fostering a new identity, that was more American than foreign among the many different nationalities that flocked to Chicago, is analyzed. The argument presented is that this role has been largely ignored by historians, yet, the Churchs' influence on the immigrants was decisive. As the mass of immigration from Catholic countries in Europe to America grew, so did the Catholic Church in the United States. Its work among the immigrants deserves recognition particularly as a factor in the acculturation and well-being of the newcomers.

117. Smith, T. L. (1978). Religion and ethnicity in America. American Historical Review, 83(5):1155-1185.

The author reviews three alterations in the relationship of faith to ethnic identity that were produced as a result of migration, 1) people-hood; 2) an intensification of the ethno-religious commitment, due to the emotional consequences of uprooting and resettlement, and 3) a revitalization of the messianic hopes for a common humanity. The faith commitments helped to define more sharply the boundaries among subcultures, while the common yearning for a hope - for unity of all humankindexceeded them, thereby leading to a dialectical relationship between religion and ethnicity.

118. Stout, H. S. (1975). Ethnicity: The vital center of religion in America. Ethnicity, 2(2):204:224.

The author cites reasons why America is moving towards a cultural religion, which is seen as a blending of Protestantism, Catholicism, and Judaism. In this cultural religion plurality and consensus form the American way. This development came about a consequence of three historical processes: 1) immigration aimed at preserving the religious totality of a particular group; 2) efforts at "Americanization", or assimilation, but with the maintenance of the basic ethnic identity; and 3) expansion of the religious associations into the civil and cultural life of the nation as a whole, contributing to the creation of a cultural religion. The process is not yet completed. The author argues in favor of a new methodology in the study of ethnicity and religion in America.

119. Vignola, S. L.   The American Jewish women's socialization process: The study of mother-daughter relationship as it affects the daughter's future choice of the husband.   Doctoral dissertation, The Catholic University of America, 1979.   Studies in Social Work, No. 129.   Dissertation Abstracts International, 40(20): 1081-A.   Order No. 7918583.

The associations between an American Jewish woman's early life experiences and her marriage to a Jewish or non-Jewish man, and such a woman's ethnic identity and continuity of Jewish ethnic values in the home she establishes, were studied with a sample of 72 women between the ages of twenty three and seventy one. These women volunteered to complete an anonymous, fixed-alternative, mailed questionnaire. A strong moderate correlation was found to exist between maternal Jewish identity, activity, warmth, and marriage to the Jewish or non-Jewish man.

120. Weiss, R. (1979). Ethnicity and reform: Minorities and the ambience of the depression years. Journal of American History, 66(3):566-585.

By the eve of World War II many Americans had begun to view ethnics and ethnic cultures in American nationality not only as positive, but as essential for the welfare of the nation. This turn about in attitudes toward the ethnics was spearheaded by the intellectuals who reacted to the racial persecutions of the Nazis, and who saw the ethnics in America as victims of the society during the depression years of the 1930's.

Health - Physical, Psychological, and Social

121. Caliandro, G. G. B. The visiting nurse movement in the Borough of Manhattan, New York City, 1877-1917. Doctoral dissertation, Columbia University, 1970. Dissertation Abstracts International, 32:1680-B.

In this historical study of visiting nursing the focus is on the emergence and development of this profession in the context of the social factors that shaped its beginnings. The great influx of immigrants to the New World, and to New York City, created a great shortage in adequate housing and health care facilities for the sick poor among the immigrants. Visiting nurses were a welcome relief. They extended the scope of medical and social care beyond the then customarily available services. Their help was particularly important in light of the fact that 90 percent of the sick poor remained at home during illness.

122. Chrisman, N. J. and Kleinman, A. (1980). Health beliefs and practices. In S.T. Thernstrom A. Orlov and O. Handlin (Eds.). Harvard Encyclopedia of American Ethnic Groups. Cambridge, MA: Belknap Press of Harvard University Press, 452-462.

This essay reviews the health beliefs and practices of American ethnic groups. Beliefs about maintaining health and curing sickness are part of the culture of any group, stem from the shared symbols and values of social conduct, and constitute the essence of the life of the group. Health beliefs vary widely among the ethnic groups in America. They influence attitudes about what is considered healthy and sick, the remedies people use in treating illnesses, and the evaluation of the efficacy of treatment.

Despite modern scientific medicine available in theory to all peoples in the United States, homeland medical cultures of immigrant groups and American folk medicine exert powerful influences on health related behaviors and practices. Medical traditions based on beliefs and practices in the country of origin carried over to the new country do not die easily. Only 10 to 30 percent of all sicknesses are treated by doctors, leaving ample room for folk healers, and most importantly, to the popular health-care system used in the family and the ethnic neighborhood. Cultural and social factors influence how people take care of their health and how they respond to sickness. They also influence the perception, labeling and communicating of symptoms and help seeking behaviors. Northern European ethnics behave very differently, for example, from Italians and Greeks, as well as Jews regarding health practitioners. Their belief in modern medicine is far greater than those of many other ethnics. Distinctive ethnic health beliefs and practices are based in strong ethnic identities and integrated ethnic group structures.

123. German, P. S., Shapiro, S., Chase, G. A. and Vollmer, M. H. (1978). Health care of the elderly in medically disadvantaged populations. The Gerontologist, 18(6): 544-555.

Three disadvantaged urban ethnic areas in Baltimore, Maryland, were selected to study the relationship between available resources and ambulatory health care. The most prevalent conditions of the elderly in these areas included arthritis, high blood pressure, and heart trouble. Over three-fifths of the sample indicated problems with physical mobility. High proportions of the elderly with serious conditions received ongoing monitory care. Highly prevalent, but less life-threatening, conditions were less likely to be treated. Many elderly, especially in transitory communities, turn to medical and health care services for problems other than their health in an attempt to maintain their independence. Implications of these findings are discussed.

124. O'Rourke, W. D.   The relationship between religiousness, purpose-in-life, and fear of death. Doctoral dissertation, The University of Nebraska-Lincoln, 1977.   Dissertation Abstracts International, 37(11-A):7046-7047, Order No. 7803881.

Christian volunteer subjects, aged 65 to 96 years, residing in a nursing home, who were judged to be alert and well oriented, were studied in relation to their religiousness, purpose-in-life and fear of death. A high degree of religiousness was thought to be associated with a high degree of purpose-in-life and less fear of death - as these would indicate an inner strength and a philosophy of life strong enough to withstand the losses accompanying old age. No relationship was found between religiousness and fear of death, but statistically significant differences were found between the high and low belief groups in the sample supporting the hypothesis that religiousness was related to higher purpose-in-life. Implications are drawn for further study.

125. Ragucci, A. T.   Generational continuity and change in concepts of health, curing practices, and ritual expression of the women of an Italian-American enclave.   Doctoral dissertation, Boston University Graduate School, 1971.   Dissertation Abstracts International, 32: 1974-B.

Folk concepts of health and healing practices were studied by method of participant-observation. The women of the first generation, or immigrants from Italy 50 to 60 years ago, comprised the baseline. Continuities and discontinuities of health and healing practices are described, and the manner in which these are expressed and reinterpreted within an urban milieu are identified.

126. Rubin, B. (1977). The role of the community center in meeting the health needs of the aged: An overview, Journal of Jewish Communal Service, 54(1):32-38.

A description of present and projected prevention health programs in community centers is presented. Such programs can preserve the happiness and dignity of Jewish aged, are less costly then nursing home care, and may be useful in preventing or delaying custodial care of the frail, isolated and depressed elderly.

Health counseling, early case finding, and home service outreach
are suggested methods for preventive health care.

Income and Income Maintenance

127. Greeley, A. M. (1976).   The ethnic miracle.   Public Interest,
45:20-36.

The economic and educational successes of Italians and Poles in
particular, and other southern and eastern European immigrants who
came to the United States before World War I, are reviewed.   The
author bases the evidence on an analysis of 12 national sample
surveys conducted by the National Opinion Research Center in
Chicago.   The present generation of Italian and Polish-American
elderly made great strides forward due to their hard work, saving,
sacrifice and close and intense parental attention to the needs of
their children.   Despite the notable success, and a higher than
average level in both income and education, college graduates
still have difficulty in entering prestigious occupations, perhaps
because of lingering discrimination against them.

128. Hill, P. J. (1975).   Relative skill and income levels of
native and foreign born workers in the United States.   Explorations in Economic History, 12(1):47-60.

One of the commonly held views about the immigrants from southern, and eastern Europe to the United States was that the great
majority of them were unskilled, and that, as a consequence, their
economic position was much lower than that of the native born, as
they were forced to enter the job market at the bottom.   This view
is challenged by the author, who reviews the period 1878-1920 com-
paring the above two groups with regard to their economic status.
His findings reveal that there were few differences between them
in terms of annual earnings and savings,   or in job skills.
Furthermore, the foreign-born had a higher rate of home ownership
than did the native-born.

129. Huberman, S. (1986).   Jews in economic distress.   Journal of
Jewish Communal Service, 62(3):197-208.

The new Jewish poverty is described using New York City and
Chicago as illustrations.   These two cities mounted comprehensive
anti-poverty projects as a response to some alarming statistics:
in New York City 13% of the Jewish population is poor, half of
them are elderly yet, 62% of poor Jews do not report contact with
Jewish agencies.   In Chicago 15% are economically disadvantaged,
and close to half of them (48%) are aged.   The majority of poor
Jewish elderly are older women.   The rate of poverty among elderly
Jews is increasing due to social welfare program cuts by the
Federal government.   At the same time philanthropy has not kept
pace with the rising need for assistance.   Ideas of what needs to
be done to avert a crisis are offered.

130. Root, L. S. and Tropman, J. E. (1984). Income sources of the elderly. Social Service Review, 58(3):384-403.

The economic situation of households headed by elderly persons is analyzed in terms of sources of income and differences associated with household size, race and gender. Over 5,000 families were selected as representative of households nationally. Of these 834 families in which the head or "householder" is 65 years or older were interviewed in 1980. The relative contribution of earnings, assets, Social Security, private pensions, and Supplemental Security Income are presented. As a group, women are poorer than men, and employed less often. A large difference exist between the incomes of Black and White aged persons, with the former having less income from earnings, assets, pensions, and Social Security. Income maintenance policies need to be altered to address the deficits of a lifetime in the later years of a person's life.

131. Serow, W. J., Spar, M. A. and Martin, J. H. (1983). Income characteristics of the European ethnic elderly: 1960-1970. In Garbacz, C. (Ed.). Economic Resources for the Elderly: Prospects for the Future. Boulder, Colorado: Westview Press, 131-148.

Using 1960 and 1970 Public Use Sample data for 22 groups of white ethnic elderly, the relationship between household income and ethnic status were explored. The high income category was dominated by eastern European ethnics, while the low income groups were primarily Scandinavians. Household size was the most important economic factor, with larger household having higher incomes. Lower incomes were noted among elderly with lower education and chief income earners.

132. Silverberg, D. (1977). The "old" poor - and the "new" - what's happening to them? Present Tense, 4(3):59-64.

The plight of American urban Jewish poor is examined through the writings of noted scholars. Government and local community sources, including those of the Hasidic Jews, are cited.

Employment and Volunteer Work

133. Beeten, N. (1976). Polish American steelworkers: Americanization through industry and labor. Polish American Studies, 33 (2):31-42.

Many of the Polish immigrants to the midwest came to Indiana to work in the United States Steel Corporation in Gary. This study refers to their experiences there covering the years 1906-1920. Use of the scheme of Americanization by the steel giant turned out to be a beneficial factor for both employer and the employees. The former gained the hard work and loyalty of the immigrants,

while the latter learned how to survive in a hard economic world.
An additional benefit to the workers was the exposure to organized
labor - including unionization.

134. Buhle, M. J. (1976). Socialist women and the "girl strik-
ers," Chicago, 1970. Signs, 1(4):1039-1051.

Garment workers in Chicago in the first decade of this century
were largely young immigrant women. They opposed the policies of
the United Garment Workers as being too conciliatory toward fac-
tory owners and went on strike in 1910. Their struggle was he-
ralded by writers of those times as a symbol of the working
classes' insistence on determining their own destiny in industria-
lizing America.

135. Davis, S. G. (1978). Women's role in a company town: New
York Mills, 1900-1951. New York Folklore, 4(1-4): 35-47.

Many Polish immigrant women worked in New York Mills, New York,
to support themselves and their families. This article traces
these women between 1900-1951 through personal reflections.
Stories told depict the many roles Polish immigrant women occupied
in addition to being employees of the mills.

136. Greene, V. (1976). The Polish American worker to 1930: The
"hunky" image in transition. Polish Review, 21(3): 63-78.

The image of Polish immigrant laborer between 1860 and 1930 was
one of a naive illiterate bumbler who used strength instead of
intellect in resolving problems at work and elsewhere. This ba-
sically negative image persisted among historians of the above
era well into the 1920s. An evolution in thought has happened
only during 1920-1960, the time frame of this study, when intellectuals and historians saw Polish immigrant laborers in much more
positive ways, as people who were able to adjust well to the new
conditions they encountered in the United States.

137. Frederick, J. T. Spar, M. A., Martin, J. H. and Serov, W. J.
(undated). "Determinants of Labor Force Participation for the
White Ethnic Elderly." Research Report, National Institute on
Aging, Grant No. 1 R01 AG0152201.

Participation in the labor force by nine elderly white ethnic
groups was studied. The 1970 Public Use Sample tapes provided the
data for this study. Groups selected were classified according to
their labor force participation as high, medium or low. Only
those born in Europe were included in the sample. Results indicated that those receiving Social Security benefits were less

likely to be in the labor force. Age and sex were also found to
be significant determinants of labor force participation. A
significant drawback in this model is the absence of information
on health status and attitudes toward retirement.

138. Hollander, E. K. and Peyser, H. (1984).   Family volunteer
support group for Jewish aged in senior housing. Journal of
Jewish Communal Service, 61(2):169-173.

Relatives, friends, and tenants working together can make a
senior adult apartment building become a functioning community.
An illustration from such a housing in Washington, D.C. is given
to describe how to activate volunteer organizations and how to
offer support and services to aged residents. The focus of the
volunteer group is on the encouragement and enhancement of independent living by the elderly, while their role is to serve as
facilitators in this process.

139. Kesser, T. and Caroli, B. B. (1978).   New immigrant women at
work: Italians and Jews in New York City, 1880-1905. Journal of
Ethnic Studies. 5(4):19-31.

This article is a historically based statistical analysis on the
role of ethnicity in shaping the occupational distribution of
women in New York City in the late nineteenth and early twentieth
centuries. Italian women's upward mobility consisted of moving
from initial unskilled to skilled blue- collar jobs. Jewish
women, on the whole, generally started at higher status levels.
Their progress was more rapid. Differences in attitudes to education and to family life were additional factors in the differential mobility patterns of Italian and Jewish women.

140. Lowell-Troy, L. A. (1981).   Ethnic occupational structures:
Greeks in the pizza business. Ethnicity, 8(1): 82-95.

Greek immigrants to the United States have followed similar
patterns of employment in different occupations since the first
wave of Greek immigration at the end of the 19th century. Recent
immigrants to Connecticut have entered the pizza business, which
is considered as a traditional Italian business catering to the
large Italian population of that state. This entrance into the
pizza business is similar to that found in other Greek businesses,
and is indicative of an economic adaptation by Greek immigrants to
changes in the American economy which affect the entire restaurant
business. The latter was among the two most prominent industries
which employed Greek immigrants since the turn of the 20th century.

Involvement in Social and Communal Affairs

141. Abramson, H. J. (1980). Assimilation and pluralism. In S.
T. Thernstrom, A. Orlow, and O. Handlin (Eds.). Harvard Encyclo-
pedia of American Ethnic Groups. Cambridge, MA: Belknap Press of
Harvard University Press, 150-160.

The processes that lead to greater homogeneity in society, and
the conditions that produce sustained ethnic differentiation and
continued heterogeneity are reviewed. Three possibilities of
assimilation as social change at many levels and stages include:
1) assimilation of individuals and/or groups of a particular
ethnic background into some form of the dominant Anglo-Saxon
Protestant ethnicity; 2) assimilation into another minority ethnic
collectivity, and 3) individuals or groups may assimilate to a
truly mixed subculture.
The heterogeneity of the American people - expressed in the
complex and dynamic term "cultural pluralism" - may be linked to
both traditionalism, or inherence to past affiliations of race,
religion, and national origin, and to the emergence of differentiated ethnic cultures and new syntheses, such as religio-ethnic
sectarianism and different forms of political ethnicity. Both
assimilation and pluralism are linked with the idea of change in a
culturally diverse society, yet, this change is not always appre-
ciated, nor understood in terms of its consequences for the individual. Issues such as group boundaries and attachments to groups
are discussed along with definitions of ethnicity, directions of
assimilation, the pluralist alternative to Anglo conformity, and
individual experience and change. Four social and cultural conditions for the individual include: 1) the presence and certainty
of both ethnic symbols and relationships; 2) the certainty of
ethnic structure but ambiguity of the ethnic culture, which is
viewed as the beginning of ethnic change; 3) social and cultural
exile of an individual or isolation with a past identification and
a memory of belonging, and 4) a lack of both ethnic culture and
ethnic structure which prevent the individual from finding his or
her roots.

142. Berger, G. (1976). American Jewish communal service 1776-
1976: From traditional self-help to increasing dependence on government support. Jewish Social Studies, 38(3-4):225-246.

Jewish immigrants to America brought with them a historical
tradition of self-help, of "taking care of their own" by the
community. This tradition was, and still is, the main factor in
the rise and development of Jewish social welfare agencies for
serving the needs of the Jewish community. Helping fellow Jews in
times of crisis, and taking responsibility for the welfare of the
community, are traits that characterize Jewish welfare philosophy
- similar to that of the various Christian denominations. Greater
dependence on the government in meeting the welfare needs of a
growing population brought a change in the provision of services,
as federal policies require a non-sectarian emphasis in social
welfare for eligibility to federal support. As a result, Jewish
agencies have assumed in the past few decades a quasi governmental
status.

143. Berger, P. L. and Neuhaus, R. J. (1977). To Empower People:
The role of Mediating Structures in Public Policy. Washington,
D.C.: American Enterprise Institute for Public Policy Research.

The role of alternative structures in providing welfarestate
services is explored in this initial report. Alternative structures considered include the neighborhood, the family, the churches and synagogues, and the voluntary associations. These legiti-
mize needed services, provide them in acceptable, democratic ways,
and reduce dependence on government bureacracies. The strength of
pluralism is stressed as a means of resisting totalitarian tendencies in policy-planning and implementation. The authors oppose
tendencies to "massification" and encourage the empowerment of the
citizens.

144. Dravich, R. B.   A comparison of the leisure attitudes of
elderly Jews and elderly non-Jews. Doctoral dissertation, University of Oregon, 1980. Dissertation Abstracts International,
41(11):4835A, Order No. 8109674.

The leisure attitudes of elderly Jews and non-Jews in Portland,
Oregon, were compared.   Subjects were drawn from two community
centers and their demographic backgrounds and characteristics
assessed. Two fifths of the Jewish elderly were foreign born, as
opposed to only 5 percent among the non-Jewish elderly in the
sample.
Attitudes to leisure were measured by 32 statements covering the
subjects' aesthetic, civic, intellectual, mass media, physical,
social and spiritual activities. No statistically significant
differences were found to exist in the categories of attitudes
toward the areas elaborated above, except in social and touristic
activities.   American born Jewish elderly differed from their
Eastern-European born peers in volunteer work and adult education
classes.

145. Friedman, H. H. (1984). Changes in programming for the
Jewish aged in residential health care facilities. Journal of
Jewish Communal Services, 60(4):324-330.

A study of the characteristics of 127 Jewish residential health
care facilities reveals a trend toward a decreasing number of
facilities with solely Jewish patients, and an increasing number
of facilities having a pluralistic patient population. At the
same time the present residents come from higher socioeconomic
levels than ever before; are better educated, and have a serious
interest for involvement in societal issues of the day. Previous
programs of activities were oriented toward "arts and crafts,"
religious services, and weekly movies. These, however, do not
satisfy the new type of residents. Changes in programming must be
undertaken to meet the cultural, educational and recreational
needs of these residents, while continuing to uphold Jewish traditions and ideals.

146. Gans, H. (1973). Ethnicity and the peer group society. In Ryan, J. (Ed.). White Ethnics: Their Life in Working Class America, Englewood Cliffs, New Jersey: Prentice-Hall, 74-81.

Acculturation of the second generation of Italian and Sicilian immigrants to American ways of life is the subject discussed in this interesting article. The author points out the durability of ethnic food habits and the Italian language among these people, while ethnic identification with Italy has almost completely disappeared.

Italian-Americans living in the West End form a peer group society within three interrelated sectors: the primary group, the secondary group and the out-group. The first of these three groups refers to that combination of family and peer relationships which the author calls the "peer group society". The community, consisting of the local Italian institutions and voluntary organizations, is the secondary group, while all non-Italian institutions in the outside world are called the outgroup. The most important part of an ethnics' life is lived in the primary group. The peer group dominates the entire life and structures the ethnic person's relationship to the outside world. Life in the peer group society exerts a pressure on all members and has far-reaching psychological and social consequences. These are elaborated vividly by the author.

147. Gleason, P. (1980). American identity and Americanization. In S. T. Thernstrom, A. Orlov, and O. Handlin (Eds.). Harvard Encyclopedia of American Ethnic Groups. Cambridge, MA: Belknap Press of Harvard University Press, 31-58.

The aim of this essay is to review historically the place of ethnicity in the tradition of thinking and writing about American identity, or what it means to be an American. The term "American identity" is employed interchangeably with "American nationality" and "American character" to reflect the indeterminacy of the phenomena to which they refer. The author cites Hans Kohn who emphasized the ideological nature of American nationalism. According to Kohn, a sense of distinctive peoplehood could be founded only on ideas, because the great majority of Americans shared language, literature, religion and other cultural traditions with the nation against which they had successfully rebelled. The foundation of nationality rests on principles of liberty, equality, and government embodied in the Constitution. The universalist ideological character of American nationality means that it is open to anyone who wills to become an American. Two additional characteristics of this nationality include newness, in terms of historical origin - which begins with the Revolution and the establishment of a unified government in the 1780s - and future orientation. The existence of American nationality does not mean that all Americans are alike, but that a genuine national community does exist - along with its history and sense of belongingness. Similarly, this nationality does not preclude the existance of ethnicity in the subgroup peoplehood-sense. Nor should subgroup ethnicities be regarded as more privileged, as having some sort of existential priority over American nationality.

148. Guttmann, D. (1985).   The social network of ethnic minorities.   In Sauer, W. J., & Coward, R. T. (Eds.).   Social Support Networks and the Care of the Elderly, New York: Springer Publishing Company, 199-218.

This chapter examines the concept of social networks that affect the elderly in different ethnic groups and the impact of these networks on social policy in aging. Social networks, ethnicity, and minority are defined, and the relationship between ethnicity and minority is discussed. Theoretical issues related to kinship and social networks are highlighted with research illustrations drawn from recent studies, including ongoing re-research on stress management, which provides an additional perspective. Ethnic minorities generally live in poverty, lack education skills to deal with bureaucracies, and often their cultural values prevent them to reap many of the benefits to which they are entitled. As a result they tend to live in ethnic enclaves and rely on the supports of their informal worlds of extended family, friends, neighbors and ethnic organizations.

149. Harrington, M. (1980). Loyalities: Dual and divided. In S. T. Thernstrom, A. Orlov, and O. Handlin (Eds.). Harvard Encyclopedia of American Ethnic Groups. Cambridge, MA: Belknap Press of Harvard University Press, 676-686.

The complex issues involved in the meaning and the practice of loyalty of immigrants to the United States are discussed. These are especially acute for some of the older European-Americans who maintain a sense of divided loyalty, among them the sojourners or political refugees, who came here with firm intention to return to the old country as soon as economic or political realities would permit. Loyalty to the homeland affects not only those who were born and raised in a country other than the United States but, also, subsequent generations. Emotional ties, active support, political and economic activities on behalf of the old homeland, even service in its armed forces, when consistent with American national interests, are expressions of such loyalty. The meaning of loyalty to the United States rests on unwavering perception of freedom guaranteed in the Constitution. This sense of freedom permits the expression of interest in the welfare of another country without renouncing the basic and the essential allegiance to the United States. Even the laws which define loyalty are subject to the great principles of individual freedom. Loss of citizenship of nationalized Americans (i.e. many of the present generation of Euro-American elderly) can occur only when there is evidence of an actual transfer of allegiance to another country.

Dual and divided loyalties have always been a problem for American ethnic groups. They are always forced to define the point at which their loyalty to the United States makes it unacceptable to maintain attachments to the homeland or to promote its causes. While the openness of the American political system encourages a multiplicity of interests, and allows groups to act on their differences, it also sets up mechanisms to smooth out differences, even to deny them. When issues of "American identity" are resolved, ethnic groups gain a sense of pride in their ancestry.

150. Higham, J. (1980). Leadership. In S. T. Thernstrom, A. Orlov and Handlin (Eds.). Harvard Encyclopedia of American Ethnic Groups. Cambridge, MA: Belknap Press of Harvard University Press, 642-647.

Three types of leadership in the ethnic community are discussed: 1) received leadership over an ethnic group; 2) internal leadership, that arises within the group and remains there, the leader being rooted in his ethnic group and addressing the external world as its representative and advocate; and 3) projective leadership, or leadership from an ethnic group, whereby an individual acquires a following outside of the group with which he or she is identified and thus affects its reputation without being subjected to its control. Leaders are seen as individuals who exercise decisive influence over others in a given social group. Leaders have been very important for maintenance of the ethnic group, but the high degree of decentralization and specialization in American society have limited the scope of leadership. European origin ethnic groups lack a distinct, assured territorial base. Hence their leaders cannot control and direct the entire ethnic group. Leaders on the local level focus on the task of making the identity of the ethnic group visible to others.

The decline of the charismatic leaders of various ethnic groups in the past has been counterbalanced by the professionalization of leadership, which is seen by the author as contributing to the stability and permanence of ethnic groups. These leaders seem to offer a relatively practical, accomodating style of leadership. Their commitment is to provide effective services while minimizing internal conflict within their groups.

151. Jacobs, J. (1974). An ethnographic study of a retirement setting. The Gerontologist, 14(1):483-487.

This article describes Fun City, a planned retirement setting somewhere in the south. Residents are white, middle-class, presumably ethnic, pre-elderly and elderly people. The life styles they lead, including their planned activities, are analyzed using disengagement theory as the conceptual basis. The aridness of the setting is matched by the aridness of the lives they are engaged in. Lack of elementary services, such as public transportation,

police or health care facilities, add to feelings of isolation.
The "heaven on earth" many retirees of Fun City expected to find
never materialized. Lessons to be learned from this experiment
for planning retirement living are discussed.

152. Monk, A. and Cryns, A. G. (1974). Predictors of voluntaristic intent among the aged. The Gerontologist, 1(5,pt.i.):425-
429.

The correlation between stated interest in community volunteer
work and personal factors, such as age, education, belief in one's
ability to serve, interest in senior citizen activity, scope of
special interests, and home ownership, were studied in a white
ethnic working-class neighborhood in Buffalo. The correlation of
age with voluntaristic intent was found to be both significant and
negative.

153. Papanek, H. (1979). Family status production: The "work"
and "non-work" of women. Signs: Journal of Women in Culture and
Society, 4:775-781.

Offering an explanation that might be applicable to immigrant
women, the author states that in groups concerned with status, a
wife's work may consist of entertaining her husband's colleagues,
or maintaining the family's standing in the community. "Family
status production" is the term used to describe such and similar
works performed by women. Family status production is possible
more in the middle classes than in the working or lower classes,
as such work can only be undertaken when the family is able to
live above the level needed for sheer survival. Attitudes toward
women's work are related to interacting social, economic, political and cultural factors. Job opportunities, income, and appropriate occupations for women are considered in relation to the
potential loss to family status when women work outside the home.

154. Pratt, N. F. (1978). Transitions in Judaism: The Jewish
American woman through the 1930s. American Quarterly, 30(5):
681-702.

A steady growth in the status of Jewish women was noted particularly in the 1920s, and 1930s, when a number of Jewish women organizations have developed programs and activities in which women
found opportunities for making significant contributions. Growth
in status was predicated on economic factors and country of origin, that is eastern or western Europe, as well as on denomina-
tional affiliation. Differences between Reform, Conservative,
Orthodox and Secular Jewish women were evident in the attainment
of social status, while the fear of assimilation into the Gentile
culture acted as an inhibiting factor.

155. Ryan, J. (Ed.) (1973). White Ethnics: Their Life in Working Class America, Englewood Cliffs, New Jersey: Prentice Hall.

The resurgence of ethnicity among working-class white ethnics is presented. The sixteen chapters included in this book provide a definition of the concepts and a description of the central factors in ethnicity, such as the family, the parish, and the neighborhood. The lifestyles and political behavior of white ethnics are highlighted. Resources and bibliography for further study are offered.

Resurgence of the new ethnicity is explained as a parallel process to the one which swept Blacks, Chicanos, and women in the 1960s. The slow erosion of old prejudices and sterotypes, along with the political and economic upheavals that accompanied this process, is well documented. Issues pertaining to cultural pluralism are explained. White ethnic Americans struggle to maintain what is precious to them, and search for ways to preserve their heritage and values. They also try to adapt to changing conditions - as do other American ethnic groups. It is that struggle which makes the new ethnicity so important for everyone.

156. Wrobel, P. (1973). Becoming a Polish-American: A personal point of view. In Ryan, J. (Ed.). White Ethnics: Their Life in Working Class America. Englewood Cliffs, New Jersey: Prentice Hall, 52-58.

This personal recollection of the childhood memories and experiences of an ethnic child in America is useful for understanding the values guiding the behaviors of white ethnics of the old generation. By neglecting to teach children their ethnic heritage, including the Polish language, the immigrant parents were trying to prepare their children to be successful as Americans.

The educational system in which the children learned reinforced the same attitude - and added to the alienation from the original culture. On the other hand, the parish and the ethnic neighborhood, in which original Polish customs were preserved, acted as reinforcers of the old culture. The conflicts created in the psyche of Polish-American children by these contradictory attitudes and practices are well illustrated, but no solutions are offered.

Intergenerational Relations

157. Atkinson, M. P., Kivett, V. R. and Cambell, R. T. (1986). Intergenerational solidarity: An examination of a theoretical model. Journal of Gerontology, 41(3): 408-416.

The intergenerational solidarity theory is based upon the premise that association, affection and consensus are significant and interdependent dimensions of a single variable. This study provided an empirical test of this theory. Subjects were 94% white, and the remaining 6% black, older rural-transitional parents with one or more children. Path analysis techniques were used in data analysis. The results showed little support for the model. Residential propinquity and mutual helping behavior were strong predictors of intergenerational association. Objective solidarity (association) and subjective solidarity (consensus and affection) are not dimensions of one construct as theorized.

158. Bankoff, E. A. (1983). Aged parents and their widowed daughters: A support relationship. Journal of Gerontology, 38(2): 226-230.

The psychological well-being of 98 recent and still grieving Caucasian widows was examined in a nationwide study of alternative help system. Social support from parents, other family members, friends and neighbors was assessed in terms of their effectiveness for these widows. Results of the study indicate that aged parents are the most crucial sources of support while the support of children is virtually ineffective. Dependency on elderly parents by the middle-aged or older children warrants more attention by social gerontologists since aged parents play a variable support role for their adult children.

159. Beleda, S. E. (1978). Intergenerational differences in patterns and bases of ethnic residential dissimilarity. Ethnicity, 5(2):91-107.

Using the 1970 census as the data base, five variables (education, income, occupation, age structure, and mother tongue) were assessed for their importance in residential dissimilarity between immigrants and native whites of native parentage, between the latter and children of immigrants or of mixed parentage, and between the first and the second generations. Mother tongue (defined as the first language learned in infancy) is found to be the most important variable, except in the case of English-speaking nationalities.

160. Berman, R. and Geis, E. (1975). Intergenerational contact: Theological and social insights. Religious Education, 70:661-675.

Sixteen single Roman Catholic college students in New York state made contacts with the residents at Riverdale Hebrew Home for the Aged. The theological and social analysis of the students' anticipation of their own aging, acceptance or rejection of old age, feelings about institutionalized care, discovery of the elderly, and concentration on a death and dying course is presented. Implications of the findings for future study are drawn.

161. Gelfand, D., Olsen, J., and Block, M. (1978).   Two generations of elderly in the changing American family.   The Family
Coordinator, 27(4):395-404.

This article is an exploration of the changes in mutual support
among generations resulting from increased life expectancy and
rapid growth of the elderly population.   Second generation children facing major age-related role shifts may not be equipped to
provide support in the economic, psychological and social arenas
for aging parents.   Service providers must understand the interaction patterns among the generations and maximize opportunities
that can strengthen these relationships.

162. Kanouse-Roberts, A. L.   A study of the inter action between a
group of Jewish senior citizens and a group of Black adolescent
girls classified as delinquent.   Doctoral dissertation, Columbia
University Teachers college, 1977.   Dissertation Abstracts International, 38(7-A): 3892.

This study was designed to explore helpful methods for over-
coming the negative effects of being known as deviants by fearful
old people.   It was anticipated that social activities in a
friendly safe setting would be possible in spite of age, race and
ethnic differences of the two groups.   Methodology employed included face-toface interactions on a daily basis for three months.
This method enabled both groups to be less fearful of each other
and more tolerant and more aware of their own and other people's
feelings and behavior.   Implications for education of both young
and old are offered.

163. Streltzer, A. (1979).   A grandchildren's group in a home for
the aged. Health and Social Work, 4(1):168-183.

This article describes a short-term group process with young
people who came regularly to the Jewish Home for the Aged in
Toledo, Ohio to visit their grandparents.   Grandchildren were seen
by the social workers there as important links between the generations for maintaining family values, traditions, and commitments,
and as valuable supports for their grandparents.   The grandchildren were organized in a group so that they could gain insight
into the behaviors of their parents and grandparents.   A comfort-
able atmosphere was created in the group which fostered trust and
knowledge about older people and about the services provided by
the home.   The quality of interaction between the generations were
enhanced through this intervention, and the extended family as a
whole was strengthened.   Social workers are urged to look upon the
family of three and four generations as the unit of treatment and
upon the grandchildren as viable partners in enhancing the quality
of life of aged residents in nursing homes.

164. Thomas, K. and Wister, A. (1984).   Living arrangements of older women: The ethnic dimension. Journal of Marriage and the Family, 46(2):301-311.

A study based on a sample of 7,015 previously married, widowed, divorced, and separated women was conducted to identify factors influencing living arrangements of these people.   The role of ethnicity was emphasized as well.   Subjects were women from the British, French, Italian, and Jewish ethnic groups.   Findings indicated that fertility and ethnicity were major factors in determining whether or not an older woman lived alone.   Older Jewish and British women were more likely to live alone than older French and Italian women.   These ethnic differences in living arrangements are attributed to cultural norms and values held by the subjects of this study.

Family and Neighborhood Support

165. Biegel, D. E. and Sherman, W. R. (1979).   Neighborhood capacity building and the ethnic aged.   In D. Gelfand and A. J. Kutzik (Eds.).   Ethnicity and aging: Theory, Research and Policy.   New York: Springer Publishing Company, 320-339.

Research conducted in a working-class, largely Euro-American ethnic neighborhood in the south side of Milwaukee, Wisconsin, as well as in Baltimore, Maryland in a similar area, was aimed to revealing where ethnic elderly go to find support for their problems.   Also studied were factors of ethnicity and community attachment as intervening variables, and the obstacles to seeking and to receiving assistance with personal problems.   Findings reveal the extent to which lack of knowledge of community resources, pride, and need for privacy act as obstacles to seeking and getting help.   Community leaders and helpers included in the sample are ignorant of the extensive resources available to the elderly. Similar findings apply to the professionals.   Thus the whole helping network is seen fragmented and ineffective.   A model combining the lay and the professional networks of assistance to the elderly in urban ethnic neighborhoods is explicated.

166. Brody, E. (1981).   "Women in the middle" and family help to older people.   The Gerontologist, 21(6):471-480.

Two major trends taking place concurrently have potential for affecting family care of the elderly: 1) the greatly accelerated rate of increase in the very old population, and 2) the large scale entry of women into the work force.   These two trends produce a phenomenon characterized by researchers at the Philadelphia Geriatric Center as "women in the middle".   Such women are middle aged, in the middle generation, and in the middle of demands for their time, energy and care.   A study with 172 such women representing nearly 20 ethnic backgrounds is presented.   The vast majority of these women endorse their traditional value of filial

responsibility to the aged. However, they would like to be assisted in their caregiving functions by formal (nonfamily) providers of services.

167. Cicirelli, V. G. (1985). The role of siblings as family
caregivers. In Sauer, W. J. and Coward, R. T. (Eds.). Social
Support Networks and the Care of the Elderly, New York: Springer
Publishing Company, 93-107.

A large proportion of the elderly have living siblings, even in
the very old category, and a significant percentage of them are
living within a hundred miles. The amount of contact expressed in
mutual visitations and the quality of the relationship between
elderly siblings are reviewed. Feelings of closeness and compat-
ibility seem to increase with the advancing years, while conflict
among siblings tends to decline. Attachment and substitution theories are offered as explanation for these findings. An important
aspect of sibling relationships is the support they provide each
other, especially in the later years. While the siblings as primary sources of help are regarded as such by a small percentage of
the elderly, occasional and supplementary help is exchanged among
a large proportion of them. Siblings may be included in the informal support network by professionals for assistance, both in
economical, psychological and emotional terms, when planning services for the elderly. Research in this rather overlooked area
of gerontology is advocated.

168. Fandetti, D. V. and Gelfand, D. E. (1976). Care of the aged,
attitudes of white ethnic families. The Gerontologist, 16(6):
544-549.

The study reported here probed the attitudes of working class
Italian and Polish-Americans toward care of aged relatives. Of
the 51 women and 49 men interviewed as the sample with similar
socio-economic characteristics, more than half indicated an interest for the elderly relative to live with family members regardless of this person's physical condition. However, an almost
equal number of respondents were willing to consider the use of
institutional care for bedridden relatives. Preference for intergenerational living arrangements was stronger among the third
generation of immigrants and among the less well educated. Implications of these findings for social policy and programming such
as cash assistance and/or tax rewards are discussed.

169. Gambino, R. (1973)). La famiglia: Four generations of
Italian-Americans. In Ryan, J. (Ed.). White Ethnics: Their Life
in Working Class America. Englewood Cliffs, New Jersey: Prentice
Hall, 42-51.

"La famiglia" for Italian-Americans of Sicilian origin is composed of all of one's "blood relative". It has been in the past, and still it is, a very different institution from the American nuclear family. Most of the Sicilian immigrants to America were contadinis, or peasants, who paid attention only to the unwritten but complex and demanding rules of the family. The simple norms governing one's relations in a system in which roles were defined from birth served as protective, as well as isolating factors. Positions of superiority and subordination were clearly designated within the family hierarchy both inside and outside of the family, and a person's identity was firmly established. The geographical position of Sicily, that of being in the crossroads of the Mediterranean, resulted in constant conquests by many nations. The contadini, as a consequence, have developed a cynical attitude toward the "outsiders" and a fierce loyalty to one's own family – la famiglia. This loyalty is challenged by the American system of democracy, and by the aspirations for success and acceptance by the second and third generation of Italian-Americans. For the old immigrants this conflict in loyalties presents a real problem. Resolution of this conflict may take different forms. So far no clear model of conflict resolution has emerged.

170. Gelfand, D. E. (1986). Assistance to the New Russian Elderly. The Gerontologist, 26(4):444-449.

A sample of 259 older Russian Jews who recently migrated to the United States and are now living in New York City constituted the respondents to this research. Attitudes toward assistance from various sources were probed by a questionnaire, which was first developed in English, translated into Russian, and retranslated by a third individual to provide a reliability check on the translation process. Group sites used for data collection do not provide a random sample of older Russian Jews, as they do not cater to isolated and poorly educated individuals or those who are averse to using formal services. However, the author believes that the opinions and problems found among the sample are not unrepresentative of the overall situation of older Russian-Jewish immigrants. Reliance on agencies for assistance was cited by 40% of the respondents as being most valuable to the new immigrant, especially initially upon entering the country. Importance of the Russian language newspapers as information sources about day-to-day life in the United States was also cited. The need to develop self-help and support groups is stressed to counter the heavy and continuing reliance by these elderly on agencies for assistance.

171. Gelfand, D. E. (1986). Families, assistance, and the Euro-American elderly. In Hayes, C. L., Kalish, R. A. and Guttmann, D. (Eds.). European American Elderly: A Guide for Practice, New York: Springer Publishing Company, 79-93.

Family assistance to elderly Euro-Americans is tied to family composition and to perception of roles. Changes in values often create conflicts among the generations. The four generation family, which is emerging in recent years in the United States, may possess more resources for assistance, but it may also generate more conflicts among its members. Competing needs and demands for attention may affect and even threaten family cohesiveness. Factors examined as central for understanding patterns of assistance include proximity of living arrangements, the life situation of the other family members, and past relationships. Problematic situations may arise with divorce, of either children or the parents themselves, and with intermarriage between individuals from different ethnic, and sometimes religious, backgrounds. These situations require readjustment in family norms and practices. They may also affect the availability of assistance to older parents or in-laws. Past relationships of family members have repercussions in the present. Issues of dependence, intimacy and confidence, and willingness to accept responsibility for care of an infirm parent, or placing him/her in a nursing home, are potential sources of conflict or of family cohesion and strength. Differential use of public services by ethnic elderly and by their children is tied to values and traditions regarding use of formal services. The recently arrived Russian Jews may have a different attitude toward services provided by the government since they come from a different social system than many other Euro-American groups.

172. Gelfand, D. E. and Fandetti, D. V. (1980). Suburban and urban white ethnics: Attitudes towards care of the aged. The Gerontologist 20(5), 588-594.

Studies focusing on aged individuals and their families living in dense ethnic communities in major American cities were emerging in research about Euro-American elderly in the late seventies. Suburban ethnic life-styles, on the other hand, were neglected. This study with a sample of 113 Italian-American men, living in a suburban "new-town" in Columbia, Maryland, compared their reliance on traditional structures of assistance to care for aged relatives with a sample of 100 Italian and Polish working class respondents in Highlandtown, Baltimore, which is a multi-ethnic working class section of the city. The purpose of the study was to learn whether traditional sources of assistance for the aged - the family, church, and ethnic organizations - were viable in suburbia, or whether Italian-Americans, upwardly mobile and middle-class, are willing to utilize institutional facilities for elderly relatives whose spouses were deceased. Differences between urban and suburban Italian-American males' attitudes toward living arrangements for ambulatory and bed-ridden relatives were noted. The former favored the aged living with the family irrespective of physical status, while the latter opted more for institutional care. Both group's willingness to accept responsibility for an aged relative was conditioned by their immigration status. The church was considered an important factor in decisions about an organizational auspice for long-term care, while the family's traditional influence was felt by both samples. The authors conclude that the move to suburbia may be indicative to changes in attitudes toward the care of the elderly among white ethnics.

173. Gelfand, D. E. and Olsen, J. K. (1979). Aging in the Jewish family and the Mormon family. In Gelfand, D. E. and Kutzik, A. J. (Eds.). Ethnicity and Aging, Theory, Research and Policy. New York: Springer Publishing Company, 206–221.

Using a historical analysis, the authors note that both of these two religio-ethnic groups have experienced persecution, and hostility, and struggle to attain the desired upward mobility. They differ, however, in their outlook on the family, and in expectations from the family, for supporting the aged. For Mormons the family is the basic social organization in the Kingdom of God. Hence the emphasis on preserving the extended family. The Mormon Temple is a central factor in family life stability and in the lives of the elderly. Some older Mormons can carry out socially respected roles within the Church, such as missionary work, Temple work, or geneology. Older Jews, who are more assimilated in the mainstream of life in American society, do not have similar roles to play. The family in both of these groups experiences changes with the resultant diminution in its ability to provide expected care for the needy elderly.

174. Guttmann, D. (1980). Response of David Guttmann. In Civil Rights Issues of Euro-Ethnic Americans in the United States: Opportunities and Challenges. Washington, D. C.: U. S. Government Printing Office, No. 629-843/6080, 198–201.

This response to papers presented to the Civil Rights Commission by Drs. Naparstek and Lopata focuses on the relationship between the neighborhood as a dynamic, living, entity and mental health. Research findings of eight different ethnic Euro-American groups indicate that the elderly see the community in which one lives as being critical in dealing with stress and for preventing premature institutionalization. The majority of Euro- American elderly studied perceived their neighborhoods as safe and desirable places, and as social environments in which one can live in dignity. This attachment to a place called home was more significant considering the fact that 90 percent of the respondents were living in ethnically mixed neighborhoods. Those who live and participate actively in the social world of the community report fewer symptoms of mental health impairment. Research that creates a new awareness of the community and the neighborhood, not as a geographical place, not as a matter of bricks and mortar, but as a critical resource in maintaining, nurturing, developing and enhancing positive mental health, is sorely needed.

175. Hanson, S. M. and Sauer, W. J. (1985). Children and their elderly parents. In Sauer, W. J. and Coward, R. T. (Eds.). Social Support Networks and the Care of the Elderly. New York: Springer Publishing Company, 41–66.

The kinship network involving children and their elderly parents is examined. Research indicates that the children may be perceived as the "hub" or the "critical core" of the extended kinship network. The factors of proximity of the elderly parents to children, the quantity and the quality of contact, the types of assistance provided to each other, attitudes to filial responsibility, and the consequences of the relationships between the generations for the physical and social well-being of the elderly parents are discussed. Having a child for support may mean a delay in institutionalization, especially when a spouse is not present. The exchange network, involving exchanges of gifts, advice, help in emergencies, and etc., have been shown to be critical to the economic well-being of many older persons. The growing "old-old" population and children over the age of 65 who have living parents are two subgroups in aging that require special attention by social scientists.

176. Hess, B. B. and Soldo, B. J. (1985). Husband and wife networks. In Sauer, W. J. and Coward R. T. (Eds.). Social Support Networks and the Care of the Elderly. New York: Springer Publishing Company, 67-92.

The focus of this chapter is on the slim majority (53%) of persons age 65 and over who in 1980 were married and living with their spouses, and were available (at least in principle) as supports to one another. Being married is especially beneficial to old males in terms of lengthened life expectancy, health, and feeling better. Women benefit from marriage in their old age as well. The married among the elderly are generally healthier, happier, and better off than their non-married counterparts. The married have easier access to and enjoy more comfort, adequate nutrition, sexual access and companionship. Marriage partners provide material, affective and instrumental support for one another. These supports are crucial at times of illness, and enhance the overall quality of life in old age.

177. Hess, B. B. and Waring, J. M. (1978). Changing patterns of aging and family bonds in later life. The Family Coordinator, 27(4):303-314.

Family sociologists and practitioners must take an unromanticized view of intergenerational relations, and examine the persistence of bonds in later life. Changes in family patterns and life styles, expressed in transition from relationships based upon obligations to that of choice, necessitate this examination. A critical review of the research literature reveals the factors which enhance or inhibit intergenerational bonds and later life satisfaction. Bonds that do persist are based on mutual respect and are the strongest of ties in parent-child relations.

178. Hoyt, D. R., and Babchuk, N. (1981). Ethnicity and the voluntary associations of the aged, Ethnicity, 8(1):6781.

Is ethnicity important as an integrative mechanism? Is there a relationship between affiliation and self-esteem and between alienation and political involvement? These were questions explored in a descriptive analysis with 1,812 white adults 18 and older residing in Nebraska. Identification with national origin, as manifested through voluntary-group membership, was the strongest among the oldest participants (75 years and older). Country of origin was perceived by this group as very important – especially for aged individuals from no English backgrounds. This perception, in turn, was expressed in higher rates of participation in voluntary associations, such as fraternal, sport, social, professional and veteran-patriotic or other groups. The authors conclude that ethnicity, rather than serving to isolate members of society, appears to provide an additional resource for interaction, and may have a positive affect upon the self concept of the aged.

179. Huberman, S. (1984). Growing old in Jewish America: A study of Jewish aged in Los Angeles. Journal of Jewish Communal Service, 60(4):314-323.

The elderly represent a larger proportion of the Jewish population than do the elderly of other ethnic and religious groups. In order to better plan for this group a more substantial data base is needed. The need to target services to those most at risk, the need for outreach, and specific program recommendations are elaborated.

180. Kulys, R. and Tobin, S. S. (1980). Older people and their "responsible others." Social Work, 25(2):138-145.

The "responsible other" is a person named by an elderly as the one who would be responsible for his or her affairs in the case of hospitalization. A study conducted with 249 respondents 70 years and over revealed that only 6 could not name such a person. Spouses and family members are the "responsible other" of the elderly. However, for about half of the sample a person different from this designation was named as the person to whom the respondent felt closest. The complexity of the interpersonal support system needs to be taken seriously when providing services to the elderly.

181. Longino, C. F. and Lipman, A. (1985). The support systems of women. In Sauer, W. J. and Coward, R. T. (Eds.). Social Support Networks and the Care of the Elderly. New York: Springer Publishing Company, 219-233.

The support available to older women is both a gerontological and a feminist issue of growing importance, as women dominate the over 70 years old population in the United States. A support system is defined as a network through which various types of support flow to the individual at its center. Using social exchange theory as the basis for reciprocal relations, i.e. duties, rights, and obligations placed on individuals in the exchange relationship, the authors examine the situations of married, spouseless, divorced, widowed, and the nevermarried older women. Substitutions for the absence of family support are cited, and current research priorities are enumerated. Long years of socialization to maintaining family and friendship ties provide many elderly women, regardless of their marital status, with larger support networks than are available to older men.

182. Lopata, H. Z. (1980).   Euro-Ethnic families and housing in urban America. In Civil Rights Issues of Euro-Ethnic Americans in the United States: Opportunities and Challenges. Washington, D.C.: U. S. Government Printing Office, No. 629/843/6080, 165-192.

Background limitations, unwillingness of the dominant society to assist, and life constraints of Euro-American people are identified by the author as sources of problems for these ethnic groups. Low educational and rural composition of the immigrants and their lack of socialization in the dominant American culture are seen as the background limitations. The unwillingness and the inability of the society to help the immigrants are the second sources of problems, while life constraints, explained as reluctance to take advantage of available resources, are the third source of problems. The author points out that most Chicago ethnics are elderly and are rather restricted in their activities. Lack of engagement outside the home is attributed to fears of being victimized or hurt. The neglect of Euro-American immigrants may have long lasting effects on future generations. New immigrants should be treated differently to avoid and to prevent the damage and to insure their rights to life with dignity in the United States.

183. Nydegger, C. N. (1983).   Family ties of the aged in cross-cultural perspective. The Gerontologist, 23(1): 26-31.

Three myths, cherished by both laymen and gerontologists in the United States, are examined; 1) a past "golden age," 2) the golden isles," and 3) "rosy families." These myths, like many others, channel our thinking - sometimes along unrealistic paths - and lead to beliefs that tend to be illusions. The first two of these myths romanticize the past as a world we have lost and portray an utopia - which has never existed. "Rosy families" were such only in fiction. Evidence marshalled by the author presents a picture in which idealized family ties of past years are accompanied by those unpleasant aspects of familial relations that we try to forget. Problems related to the dependency of the aged on their kin and on society are discussed from an anthropological perspective, along with mechanisms used by the aged to ensure support during their years of frailty. There is a need for a realistic assessment of these relations in terms of their cost to both parents and to children trying to live out a myth.

184. Rosenthal, C. J. (1986).   Family supports in later life:
Does ethnicity make a difference?   The Gerontologist, 26(1):19-24.

Three models of aging in ethnic families related to three conceptions of ethnicity are discussed: 1) ethnicity as culture (of
the immigrants); 2) ethnicity as a determinant of social inequali-
ty, and 3) ethnicity as synonymous with traditional ways of thinking and behaving.   The first model suggests that ethnic families
lose their distinctiveness over time.   The second asserts that
social class accounts for most of the apparent differences, while
the third views ethnic families as more supportive to the elderly
than the Anglo families.   The dimensions of culture, structure,
and behavior must be kept conceptually and analytically distinct.
The analysis of the relationship between any two of these dimensions must control for the effects of the third dimension.   The
implications of each of these models for research and practice are
discussed.

185. Siemaszko, M. (1980).   Kin relations of the aged: Possible
consequences to social service planning.   In C. L. Fry (Ed.).
Aging in Culture and Society. Brooklyn, New York: J. F. Bergin
Publishers Inc., 253-271.

The kin networks of a sample of Polish Americans in Chicago are
compared to known American and Polish samples.   Differences found
are related to use of social services.   The cohort of Polish
American elderly investigated is distinctive in that the effects
of the Diaspora of World War II are becoming more and more apparent among them.   The author points out that people become more
heterogeneous as they age, and cannot be forced into the melting
pot.   Consequently, no one plan of action to resolve all problems
is suitable.   Effective social services should be planned with
cultural sensitivity to diversity among the aged and with the
knowledge of resources people have.   Receptivity to different
kinds of assistance needs to be explored as well, along with
knowledge of the circumstances under which some people are forced
to live.

186. Simos, B. G. (1973).   Adult children and their aging parents.
Social Work, 18(3):78-85.

A sample of fifty Jewish adult children reporting on sixty aging
parents, who lived in the greater Los Angeles area, revealed that
the children were intensively involved in helping their parents
cope with a wide range of problems.   Lack of recreational facilities and inadequate public transportation contributed to the
isolation of many parents.   The mere presence of the children when
visiting was perceived by the elderly as emotionally supporting,
even when there was little or no communication.   These findings
have implications for social work with all aged persons, for as
professionals social workers have to deal with physical, social
and emotional needs and problems of the elderly.

187. Vinick, B. H. (1978).   Remarriage in old age.   The Family
Coordinator, 27(4):359-364.

Increase in remarriage among people 65 and over has been dramatic in the last two decades, yet remarriage as an alternative life-
style in old age is still one of the least researched area. This
study reports on 24 remarried couples who were interviewed in
their homes three times. The purpose was to identify the situa-
tional and personal factors associated with remarriage in old age.
Findings indicate that the majority of the remarried described
themselves as being satisfied.   Those who felt unhappy thought
that they were "forced" into the marriage because of external
circumstances.   Remarriage seems to be a positive element in the
lives of the elderly and its advocacy by practitioners is urged.

188. Warach, B. (1986).   Supportive services in housing for the
elderly: Emerging needs and problems. Journal of Jewish Communal
Service, 62(4):299-306.

Development of housing at affordable rent and with adequate and
appropriate supportive services are major objectives of Jewish
services for the aged.   The great increase in the proportion of
the old (75 years and over) and especially of the very old (85
years and over) pose a special problem from managers of housing
complexes for the elderly.   Supportive services within these
complexes were geared mainly to the well elderly.   They were
designed as community facilities and not as nursing or group home
services.   Major problems of aging housing facility residents
include chronic illness, physical impairment and mental disability.   Social workers have been reasonably successful in assisting
the chronically ill and the homebound and physically impaired
elderly, but assisting the mentally impaired elderly is far more
difficult.   Often there is no choice but to turn to the courts.
While both tenants and their families look upon the housing facility as preferable to any other living arrangement, sponsors of
housing for the elderly face the inescapable problems of gradual
conversion of community housing into homes for the aged, especially for the very old, as the need for more and more supportive
services for these people change the character of housing for the
elderly.

189. Weiner, M. (1986).   Group treatment with aged.   Journal of
Jewish Communal Service, 62(4):307-317.

Group treatment with the aged is seen not as substitute for
missing relationships and defective social linkages in the lives
of the aged.   Rather, group treatment is a partial compensation
for some deficit in the life of an aged client.   Aging is perceived by the author as a developmental phase in which the aged
person must adjust to changes that are inevitable in a positive
way.   Diminution of independence and loss of control over one's
environment and social status are connected losses.   If work is

not available, adequate family relations can support a continuous sense of self. Validation of the self may come from one's reference group as well. For many aged persons it is easier to relate to one's cohort than with others, for shared memories, language and customs are part of being in a cohort. The type of group treatment used in the Jewish family services of Detroit is based on a psychodynamic model in which relationships and processes provide the "growth medium". Clients are helped to recognize, identify and express feelings. The goal is to change patterns of behavior that interfere with the individual's sense of self-worth and productive use of self in relationships.

190. Woehner, C. E. (1978). Cultural pluralism in American families: The influence of ethnicity on social aspects of aging. The Family Coordinator, 27(4):329-339.

This article looks at ethnic variations in the structure of the nuclear family, interdependence between generations, and the relationship between the family and the wider society. Older Americans in all European origin groups are either immigrants or the children of immigrants. The older person's social integration cannot be understood by looking objectively at his activities and interactions. Rather, there is a need for awareness of the meaning older people find in activities and in relationships.

191. Zeff, D. (1976). The Jewish aging: Problem dimensions, Jewish perspectives, and the unique role of the family agency. Journal of Jewish Communal Service, 53(1):81-87.

Jewish elderly are largely hidden and are not capable of militant advocacy on their behalf. They are also among the poorest, sickest, loneliest and fastest growing group in the Jewish population. Social planning committees should focus their attention on these people, while Jewish family agencies are requested to serve as advocates, helping them use to the full their government entitlements.

Educational, Recreational,and Artistic Activities

192. Berman, R. U. (1981). A Judaic journey creates communication; in-service education of staff of a Jewish home for the aged. Journal of Jewish Communal Service, 58(1):61-66.

The importance of religion in late life has been recognized by gerontologists. Studies done in this area of life have shown a significant correlation between life satisfaction and religious activity. Religious education of the staff is necessary to increase their knowledge of customs and traditions and for facilitating greater communication between employees and residents. A training program for staff, initially requested by the licensed practical nurses, is described. Content included knowledge of

Jewish holidays and festivals; attitudes to major social issues,
and to important historical events such as the Holocost, and the
establishment of the State of Israel. The training program was
found to be helpful in destroying prejudices, myths, and stereotypes.

193. Guttmann, D. (1973).   Leisure-time activity interests of
Jewish aged. The Gerontologist, 13(4):219-223.

Eastern-European and American born and raised elderly Jews have
different interest in the activities offered them by community
centers due to their cultural upbringing.   The former is more
oriented toward groups and social clubs, while the latter prefers
more individual, or solitary type activities. An understanding of
these and other differences among aged within the same religious
and ethnic group is important before planning programs for them.

194. Guttmann,   D. (1986).   Serving the needs of Euro-American
elderly through research.   In Hayes, C. L., Kalish, R. A. and
Guttmann, D. (Eds.).   European-American Elderly: A Guide for
Practice. New York: Springer Publishing Company, 230-249.

This chapter identifies and discusses issues in research about
serving the needs of the Euro-American elderly.   Research is
defined as an endeavor aimed at discovering, substantiating, and
assessing the needs of these people and the ethnic community for
providing supports to their older members.   Gaps identified in
research fall into four areas: 1) acquisition of basic knowledge
about the condition of the elderly in each and every ethnic group
in the United States; 2) ways and means open for ethnic communities in alleviating those needs; 3) knowledge of government and
public supports, and 4) issues of adequate criteria in measurement
of services.

4
Problems, Needs, and Services

Problems and Needs of Euro-American Elderly

195. Natow, A. B. and Heslin, J. A. (1982). Understanding cultural food practices of elderly observant Jews. Journal of Nutrition for the Elderly, 2(1):49-55.

Elderly observant Jews, usually Orthodox, but can belong to Conservative, and even Reform groups, live according to traditional beliefs and religious practices. Observant Jews have special food requirements. An explanation of the Jewish dietary law, or Kashrut, is given along with suggestions of how these practices may be adhered to, or what specific dietary modifications needed to provide quality health care and nutrition. Explanations of food products and consideration for institutional feeding are addressed.

196. Newman, J. M. (1985). Cultural, religious and regional food practices of the elderly. Journal of Nutrition for the Elderly, 5(1):15-22.

Food practices of the elderly are closely tied to their cultural identity, acculturation, and processes of psychocultural and behavioral change. In contrast to other aspects of life, little is known about the variation in food practices found within ethnic groups, religious groups and even regional groups. Lack of specific knowledge leaves many questions unanswered. Exploring food preferences and related issues enriches the knowledge of health care providers, social workers and others who work with the elderly, adds to the limited number of documented materials specific to ethnic populations, and helps remove prejudices and biases of behaviors not properly interpreted or understood.

197. Shanas, E. (1984). Old parents and middle-aged children: The four and five generation family. Journal of Geriatric Psychiatry, 17(1):7-19.

A quiet revolution is taking place in the United States: four
and five generation families are becoming more common.   Already
among those aged with children, one of every two is a great g-
randparent.   The new "status" of being great, or great-great
grandparent often results in consequences not anticipated ever
before, as only in this century people in general have attained
ages well above the Biblical three scores and ten.   The lack of
role models upon whom the present middle and older aged can model
their own behavior creates problems in family relationships.
Whose well-being comes first?   This is the central problem faced
by middle-aged children, and especially by women, as these are the
main sourceS of instrumental support to aged parents.   Forced to
deal with the problem on their own, the aged in general, and
Euro-American elderly among them, are learning new life-styles and
new roles as they accommodate to a society in which four and five
generations are the norm.

198. Warach, B. (1982).   Frontiers of service to the aging.
Journal of Jewish Communal Service, 59(1):26-34.

The challenges lying ahead for Jewish communities in America to
meet the needs of a vastly increased elderly Jewish population are
described.   The need to develop comprehensive services based on
close coordination between health agencies, community centers, and
other institutions is stressed.   Six frontiers in communal services for the aged are cited: 1) a commitment to a program of
advocacy in the public area on behalf of the elderly; 2) renewal
of a planning effort by agencies to assess the status of the
elderly and to develop new programs; 3) organizing an educational
program for the Jewish community on "growing older;" 4) adequate
provision of social work services for the elderly under Jewish
communal auspice; 5) development of comprehensive diagnosis,
case-management, coordinated home care, and protective services
for the chronically disabled, and 6) development of home care
services for the impaired elderly.

Services Utilization

199. Adelson, G., Kaminsky, P. and Cohen, C., (1979).   Volunteers
can help patients adjust.   Health and Social Work, 4(1):184-199.

Trained volunteers provide valuable services to aging patients
who are moving from an acute-care to a long-term care facility.
These patients often feel abandoned by their family and the acute-
care facility and are terrified at the change awaiting them.   The
Long Island Jewish-Hillside Medical Center has developed a program
in which trained volunteers act as friendly visitors and as liai-
son between the patient and the facility or community agency,
easing the pains of the transition for the elderly patient to the
long-term care facility.

200. Biegel, D. E. (1980). Response of David E. Biegel. In Civil Rights Issues of Euro-Ethnic Americans: Opportunities and Challenges. Washington, D. C.: U. S. Government Printing Office, No. 629-843/6080, 312-318.

Taking a different approach from the one cited by Rosenberg at the Consultation of the U. S. Civil Rights Commission, the author focuses on strengthening the entire range of community and social support systems in ethnic communities and linking them with professional services. Family, friends, neighbors, co-workers, clergy, neighborhood organizations, and mutual aid groups can all provide meaningful assistance in times of need to elderly Euro-Americans and to others. These people are part and parcel of the rubric of community support systems. They are capable of providing help in a culturally acceptable manner, without stigma or loss of pride. Informal community support systems could be effective to the elderly through a detailed knowledge of community strengths and by the ability of the community residents to know what will work in their particular community. This knowledge in turn will prevent duplication of effort by the professionals, or to a weakening of existing resources in the community.

201. Biegel, D. E., Naparstek, A. J. and Khan, M. M. (1982). Social support and mental health in urban ethnic neighborhoods. In Biegel, D. E. and Naparstek, A. J. (Eds.). Community Support Systems and Mental Health, New York: Springer Publishing Company, 21-36.

The relationship between social support, mental health, and life stress in urban white ethnic communities was studied. Settings comprised of the south side of Milwaukee, Wisconsin, and southeast Baltimore, Maryland. These communities consist of white, working-class ethnic neighborhoods mostly from Southern and Eastern Europe. The sample of 400 subjects consisted of 27 percent first and second generation ethnics and about 26 percent elderly. Data were collected in 1977 by trained interviewers. Results indicated that social support is indeed a positive mental health resource, even at low levels of stress. The importance of neighborhood attachment in white urban ethnic communities transcends racial and cultural differences, as recent research on other ethnic groups indicate. Neighborhood is more important in the lives of the elderly, than for other age groups.

202. Blouin, F. X., Jr. (1979). For our mutual benefit: A look at ethnic associations in Michigan. Chronicle, 15 (2):12-15.

The roles of voluntary mutual aid societies between 1850-1950 in Michigan are reviewed in this article. These mutual aid societies provided cultural, spiritual, and monetary support for many ethnic groups, including the Italians, Polish, Scandinavian, and German-Americans, and were helpful in easing the traumas of acculturation to American ways of life.

203. Gelfand, D. E. and Gelfand, J. R. (1982). Senior centers and support networks. In Biegel, D. E., and Naparstek, A. J. (Eds.). Community Support Systems and Mental Health. New York: Springer Publishing Company, 175–189.

Multi-purpose senior centers offer a variety of services and activities to the elderly in education, health, nutrition, social work, employment, recreation and creative arts. They also offer security, a sense of belonging, and improved self-image, which increases the mental health of the older member. Senior centers serve a number of support system functions, and help to strengthen informal support systems of the elderly. Providing a setting for informal contacts, opportunities for development of intimate relationships, a sharing atmosphere, and a network of informal help, individuals are helped to weather losses and to avoid isolation or depression.

Problems associated with elder abuse in families, and negative behaviors of certain social networks which can be detrimental to the efforts of the staff to foster mental health among members of the senior center, are discussed. The center's potential for positive support depends largely on the staff's ability, attitudes, training and use of resources.

204. Harel, Z. (1986). Ethnicity and aging: Implications for service organizations. In Hayes, C. L., Kalish, R. A. and Guttmann, D. (Eds.). European-American Elderly: A Guide for Practice. New York: Springer Publishing Company, 145–162.

Well-being and service needs of Euro-American elderly are reviewed. Literature cited indicates that all ethnic elderly, and not only the poor, need services. These services should foster a feeling of continuity in the lives of the ethnic elderly and lead to a strengthening of their ethnic heritage. Health care related services are not utilized according to needs because ethnic elderly prefer to receive assistance from their families. They also are suspicious of outsiders. These cultural attitudes often leave many ethnic elderly isolated, both physically and mentally.

Vulnerability of the isolated ethnic elderly should pose a grave concern for services providers. Among the steps advocated for professionals working with ethnic elderly are more effective dissemination of information about benefits and services to which all aged people in this country are entitled; creation of linking mechanisms between benefits offices, service agencies, and the ethnic elderly; support for the informal caregivers in the community; enhancement of the ability of ethnic groups to serve as mediators to services providers; and greater efforts to meet the needs of the unaffiliated elderly, especially those among them who do not have the benefit of an informal support system.

205. Harel, Z. and Harel, B. B. (1978). Coordinated services for older adults in the Jewish community, Journal of Jewish Communal Service, 54(3):214–219.

Changes in the older adult Jewish population in terms of size, economic, social and health characteristics, and vulnerability to environmental stress are noted. These changes lead to a greater reliance on formally organized services on the part of the older person. Planning, development, and delivery of services for older members of the Jewish community need to be more comprehensive. Coordination among Jewish agencies serving the aged, broad community representation on planning boards, and involvement of the older service consumers are seen as remedies in dealing with the needs of the aged.

206. Hayes, C. L. (1986). Resources and services benefiting the Euro-American elderly. In Hayes, C. L., Kalish, R. A. and Guttmann, D. (Eds.). European-American Elderly: A Guide for Practice. New York: Springer Publishing Company, 180-197.

This chapter identifies resources in the ethnic community that can strengthen the capacity of the elderly to care for themselves. It describes programs and public resources that can be utilized for this purpose, such as the ethnic media, and major newspapers in ethnic languages; the natural helpers, who provide assistance on a voluntary basis; private business; members of religious bodies and the churches.

Services benefiting the Euro-American elderly should be based on a philosophy of self-reliance and contribution to others by the elderly themselves. Creativity in use of available communal resources is advocated. Successful programs cited include Senior Ethnic Finds, in Cleveland Ohio; bilingual outreach services to the ethnic elderly in Detroit; advocating for the needs of the elderly and political action by the United Polish American Services in Philadelphia; the nutrition program called Eating Together in Baltimore, and other innovative programs in housing and in education. These programs demonstrate the ability of ethnic groups to use private and public resources efficiently and appropriately for furthering efforts at self help, and they may serve as models for those interested in providing services to ethnic elderly, including the government.

207. Hayes, C. L. and Burr, J. J. (1986). The role of government in providing support for the Euro-American elderly. In Hayes, C. L., Kalish, R. A. and Guttmann, D. (Eds.). European-American Elderly: A Guide for Practice. New York: Springer Publishing Company, 163-179.

While Americans are the most diverse society racially, culturally, ethnically and regionally, and while there should be a tolerance, if not pride and encouragement, for this diversity, government has done little to recognize the unique cultural and linguistic needs of the elderly within the many ethnic groups. Legislation targeted at benefitting limited English speaking ethnic elderly with services have not been enforced by government, nor are recognized needs to these people met adequately. A lack

of an advocating body to lobby and fight for the enforcement of
mandated benefits for Euro-American elderly is seen by the authors
as a hindrance to achieving equality with other minority groups
among the elderly population. A national coalition of Euro-
American elderly is needed to gain recognition by government for
the concerns of these people, and the political process, involving
the leadership of the ethnic community, is advocated.

208. Hayes, C. L. and Guttmann, D. (1986). The need for collaboration among religious, ethnic, and public service institutions.
In Hayes, C. L., Kalish, R. A. and Guttmann, D. (Eds.). European-American Elderly: A Guide for Practice. New York: Springer
Publishing Company, 198-211.

Religious and ethnic community insitutions play a central role
in the lives of the Euro-American aged. Ethnic leaders in particular have a vital stake in furthering collaboration. They can
also provide needed information to both the elderly members of the
ethnic community and to their families on how to gain access to
services. Efforts in collaboration should include the sharing of
certain resources, developing common objectives, and coordinating
services for homebound elderly. Barriers to collaboration need to
be identified and eliminated whenever possible. The main elements
of a working model for collaboration proposed in the article
consist of the following: development of a small working group;
formulation of a need/resource plan; preparation of a strategy for
accomplishing stated goals; organization of a program, and its
monitoring for continued support.

209. King, S. (1977). Counseling the young elderly: A responsive
approach, Journal of Jewish Communal Service, 54 (1):26-31.

The "young elderly" are persons in their 60's and early 70's,
who have very different characteristics and needs from individuals
in their late 70's, 80's or 90's. At times, and with increasing
frequency, the young elderly may even represent a different generation within the same family. This paper describes the work of
the Jewish Family Service in Los Angeles with a special "store-
front" operation. Three programs are outlined as methods of
counseling particularly appropriate for use with many younger
elderly clients. These are: 1) the Jewish family life development group; 2) the "coping group", and 3) the insight oriented
therapy group.

210. Kogut, A. B. (1970). The charity and organization societies,
the settlements and national minorities in the progressive era.
Doctoral dissertation, Columbia University, 1970. Dissertation
Abstracts International, 33:5830-A.

The Progressive Era of the late 19th century was the formative period of modern social work. Immigrants who streamed into the New World by the hundred thousands were met by the newly formed Charity Organization Societies and settlements, whose bases of operation were the large urban areas. These organizations were also helpful to a lessor degree, to Negroes migrating from the South to the North. The policies and programs of the Charity Organizations and settlements in the field of intergroup relations and social work functions and services are identified and evaluated in this study.

211. Kraus, H. P. (1970). The settlement house movement in New York City, 1886-1914. Doctoral dissertation, New York University, 1970. Dissertation Abstracts International, 31:1727-A.

Settlement houses were the first to welcome the European immigrants in America. Founded as a movement in England by Canon Samuel A. Barnett to narrow the gap between rich and poor in the emerging complex industrial world in England, and adopted by Stanton Coit, the founder of New York's Neighborhood Guilt in 1886, settlement houses quickly spread in the United States. University educated middle class workers came to the slums and ghettos of the greatly expanding cities to live and assist the newcomers by providing education and stimulation to the masses. These altruistic settlement workers were largely motivated by Protestant religious and ethical obligations to serve the less fortunate. Their purpose was to help the immigrants' adjustment to American ways of life without rejecting their deeply ingrained values and behaviors. The services provided did much to alleviate the poor conditions in which the immigrants found themselves upon their arrival.

212. Pargament, K. I. (1982). The interface among religion, religious support systems, and mental health. In Biegel, D. E. and Naparstek, A. J. (Eds.). Community Support Systems and Mental Health. New York: Springer Publishing Company, 161-174.

Greater understanding of the role social support systems play in the enhancement of mental health has been the focus of much research at present. Yet, the role of religion and of religious support systems in assisting individuals to deal with crises of daily living have been largely neglected. This article discusses the impact of religion on mental health as closely intertwined elements in well-being of people. Religious rituals, educational and counseling programs, and community activities are seen by the author as opportunities to affect others and to assist them in dealing with life crises and problems in living. Miscommunication and mistrust between the mental health and the religious communities are cited and appropriate remedies offered.

213. Rosenberg, M. L. (1980).   Ethnicity and social services:
Some policy perspectives.   In Civil Rights Issues of Euro-Ethnic
Americans in the United States: Opportunities and Challenges.
Washington, D. C.:   U. S. Government Printing Office, No. 629-843/
6080, 297-312.

Policy makers in the 1980s and later will have to confront a
great demand for social services from all segments of American
society, including elderly Euro-Americans.   A fast growing aging
population, and especially persons over 75 years of age, are most
likely to be among those in greatest need for services to cope
with the loss of spouses and friends, to help them find new goals
in life after retirement and to preserve their mental health.   The
increasing needs of the population require a reexamination of public policies aimed at the family and the elderly.   Consideration
must be given to issues that bear directly on the relationship
between ethnicity and service delivery.   Impersonal bureaucracies
that are stigmatized because of association with public welfare,
and services with elaborate intake procedures and means tests
cannot be effective in delivering personal social services for
Euro-Americans.   Many of these people come to this country to
escape tyranny and religious persecution, have a strong tradition
of self-reliance, are suspicious of public welfare, and tend to
view governmental bureaucracies with distrust.   Serving these
clients is possible only when the service is based on an intimate
knowledge of their lifestyles and value systems.

214. Silverstein, N. M. (1984).   Informing the elderly about
public services: The relationship between sources of knowledge
and service utilization.   The Gerontologist, 24(1):37-40.

Many elderly people need health and welfare services, but paradoxically, many elderly underutilize available resources, or use
them selectively.   The critical role of information in service use
was examined with 706 men and women 60 years of age and over in
Boston.   Subjects were selected by systematic probability sampling
and included the major ethnic groups in the city according to
their proportions in the total elderly population of the nation.
Knowledge of services depends on the source of information.
Generally, most respondents learned of services through the media
or through informal sources.   Implications of these findings for
information - referral services, outreach, and inclusion of the
informal network in dissemination of knowledge about services are
discussed.

Special Problems

215. Galey, M. E. (1977).   Ethnicity, fraternalism, social and
mental health.   Ethnicity, 4(1):19-53.

Southern and eastern European immigrants were helped by fraternal organizations they created to withstand the pains of assimila-

tion to their new environment. Encompassing a period of 70 years, from 1900 to 1970, and 14 ethnic groups in Pittsburgh, Pennsylvania, this article reviews and examines the many activities of these organizations on behalf of the immigrants. Of particular interest is the list of services offered, and their implications for contemporary health care. Benefits given at times of crisis, such as sickness, disability, and death, were very helpful in maintaining mental health. Self-help programs promoted not only feelings of independence but ethnic belonging and communal life, while the stigma attached to mental illness prevented the provision of mental health services to the immigrants.

216. Getzel, G. S. (1982). Helping elderly couples in crisis. Social Casework, 63(9):515-521.

Marital bonding and spousal caregiving are significant resources in old age. However, chronic impairment and illness often place heavy demands on elderly spouses in meeting caregiving expectations and day-to-day needs. The Natural Support Program (NSP) developed by the Community Service Society of New York City is aimed at exploring the value of providing an innovative service, including a range of social services and cash benefits, to caregivers for elderly relatives in the community. The impact of the caregiving function on the marital relationship of older couples is illustrated with case descriptions and analysis.

217. Harel, Z. (1981). Quality of care, congruence and well-being among institutionalized aged. The Gerontologist, 21(5):523-531.

The importance of quality of care and person-environment congruence in determining the subjective well-being of older persons in institutions for the aged were studied in Metropolitan Cleveland with a non-random sample of 125 respondents. Subjects ranged in age from 54 to 97, with an average of 80 years, were of mixed racial and ethnic backgrounds, with more than half of them living in their facilities more than a year. Findings highlight the importance of continuing ties with people, having personal responsibilities, and gratification of social needs in determining life satisfaction and satisfaction with treatment in institutions for the aged. Suggestions for the staff, for family members and friends of the residents are offered.

218. Johnson, E. S. (1981). Older mothers' perceptions of their child's divorce. The Gerontologist, 21(4):395- 401.

There has been relatively little research regarding the effects of divorce on the parents of the divorcing couple. This study, carried out in the Boston area in Longwood, where the majority of the population is middle-class and ethnic (primarily Jewish, Italian, Irish and Yankee) is based on the experiences of 212

mothers with a divorced child. Most mothers found the divorce of
the children upsetting, even years after the event occured.
Divorce of a child was seen as stressful, traumatic, and stig-
matizing, while remarriage of the children had brought them some
peace. It is probable that the divorce of a child has some negative impact on the parent's overall quality of life.

219. Harris, P. B. (1979). Being old: A confrontation group with
nursing home residents. Health and Social Work, 4(1):153-166.

Group experience offers the elderly a chance for therapeutic
ventilation, a chance to evaluate their own situation in life in
terms of others in comparable situations and personal growth.
Elderly residents at the Detroit Jewish Home for the Aged were
encouraged to form a group in order to express their feelings,
fears and problems. The group was led by a social worker. An
occupational therapist led the discussion on health related subjects. There were twenty sessions in all, but only a small number
of the residents took advantage of the group experience. These
were people with higher levels of social interaction and functioning than the rest of the residents. Main problem areas addressed in the discussions included physical and mental health,
social and financial resources, and independence versus dependence. The group process, and especially the sharing and the
support experienced by the residents helped them grow and change.

220. Kivett, V. R. (1978). Loneliness and the rural widow. The
Family Coordinator, 27(4):389-394.

A sample of 103 rural widows aged 65 to 99 years was interviewed
in North Carolina. The purpose of the study was to determine if
rural widows could be classified into three levels of loneliness
on the basis of one or more of 16 physical, social and psychological variables. Two-fifths of these women were black, and the
rest white. A pervasive sense of loneliness, with poverty, poor
health, emptiness and futility as accompanying ills of their
social status was experienced in varying frequencies by three out
of four older rural widows surveyed. The need to provide appropriate reference groups, preventive and corrective health measures, and development of accessible and flexible transportation
are discussed.

221. Krause, C. A. (1979). Ethnic culture, religion, and the
mental health of Slavic-American women. Journal of Religion and
Health, 17:298-307.

The relationship between ethnicity, family structure, and mental
health is explored in an oral history project. The three generations of Slavic women studied exhibited a remarkable degree of
mental and emotional well-being, which the author attributed to

strong family structure and to deeply internalized religiosity.
Why the Italian and Jewish women also studied did not exhibit
similar characteristics is not addressed, but in another publication cited in this bibliography a reason given indicates that
Slavic women interviewed may have been more stoic about their
lives. Also not settled is the question whether Slavic women's
mental health is a function of a supportive family system, or
whether some other variables are at work in producing this phenomenon.

222. Lawton, M. P., Kleban, M. H. and Singer, M. (1971). The aged
Jewish person and the slum environment. Journal of Gerontology,
26(2):231-239.

This research was done at the Philadelphia Geriatric Center and
was aimed at filling the existing gap in knowledge concerning
environmental factors that affect the well-being of the elderly.
Setting for the study was a once prosperous and large section of
the city that housed Jewish people and has deteriorated into a
slum, leaving behind many elderly poor Jews who immigrated primarily from Eastern European countries. Their deprived status and
the causes of their predicaments are discussed in terms of environmental influences, including selective migration and unfortunate circumstances intrinsic to aging.

223. Lopata, H. Z. (1978). The absence of community resources in
support systems of urban widows. The Family Coordinator, 27(4):
383-388.

In 1976 there were 10 million widows in the United States. Many
of them are elderly foreign born who live within quite restricted
life spaces because they lack the personal resources needed to organize their own support networks. A study of widows in Chicago
is used as illustration to document the failure of community
resources in providing support for these women. In the absence of
such support, elderly widows are dependent upon their children.
Neighbors, work associates, and club members are additional resources of support to widows in building a new life. Recommendations to family counselors and mental health specialists center on
the need for these professionals to become actively involved in
succoring help to widows.

224. Lucks, H. C. (1981). Widow/widower outreach program (WWOP):
The social work role with members of mutual-help program and their
families. Social Work Papers, 16: 82-89.

Widowed volunteers under the supervision of a social worker
function as outreach personnel to the newly widowed elderly in the
Jewish community of San Francisco. The volunteers offer emotional
support and connect the newly widowed to the program. Expanding

the friendships of these people with elderly in similar circumstances, and a supporting social network, may be valuable in confronting the variety of changes that widowhood brings to an individual and in preventing social isolation. The program offers consistency and structure to a population in a transitional crisis and helps relieving individual and family stresses resulting from widowhood.

225. Markson, E.W. (1979). Ethnicity as a factor in the institutionalization of the ethnic elderly. In D. Gelfand and A. Kutzik (Eds.). Ethnicity and Aging: Theory, Research and Policy. New York: Springer Publishing Company, 341-356.

The relationship between ethnicity and referral for mental hospitals was explored using the hospital records of 333 men and women 65 years and older. Elderly referred for psychiatric hospitalization in New York City were found to contain a disproportionate number of foreign born aged as compared to the general population. Most overrepresented were the elderly born in Eastern and in Central Europe. Low educational and occupational levels were noted for these groups of ethnic elderly, who are seen by the author as victims of the mobility trap, especially of their children. Pathways to the mental hospitalization of the elderly white poor include breakdown in family support, death of a significant other, and, at times, commitment of the primary caregiver, (i. e. the adult child living with the elderly parent) to an institution. Mental hospitalization is seen by destitute families as a cheap long term care. The isolation felt in such institutions by older ethnics is documented in moving stories along with the problems of trying to homogenize the "unmeltable" ethnics.

226. McCourt, K. (1980). Euro-ethnic women: Some observations. In Civil Rights Issues of Euro-Ethnic Americans in the United States: Opportunities and Challenges. Washington, D. C.: U. S. Government Printing Office, No. 629-843/6080, 342-360.

The focus of this paper is on working-class women of Euro-ethnic background who are the maJOR concern due to their numbers and economic situation. These women are living in families with incomes above poverty but well below affluence, have never made it through colleges, and are the daughters and granddaughters of immigrant women who struggled and saved for the survival of their families. Working-class women are traditional people. They adhere to traditional values of family and religion. They are the defenders of their cultural traditions, the pillars of the ethnic neighborhood. They also put personal fulfillment and self-actualization, cherished by middle-class women, behind their interest in the welfare of their families and neighborhoods. Loss of the community and the breakdown of their social networks are especially traumatic experiences for them. Elderly women in particular suffer a great deal when their children are moving away and when they are left in loneliness and isolation. Their problems are similar to the problems faced by all women, except that they were shaped by historical tradition and social class. Many of their problems could be resolved on the community level, if the community would remain stable, viable, secure, and economically strong, offering opportunities for employment and maintaining activities that enhance the integrity of the ethnic family.

227. Owan, T. C. (1982). Neighborhood-based mental health: An approach to overcome inequities in mental health services delivery to racial and ethnic minorities. In Biegel, D. E. and Naparstek, A. J. (Eds.). Community Support Systems and Mental Health Practice, Policy, and Research. New York: Springer Publishing Company, 282-300.

Differential mental health treatment based on race and ethnicity, underutilization, noncompliance with the Civil Rights Act of 1964, and premature termination of the psychotherapeutic treatment are cited, and supported with research, as factors that lead to inequities in mental health services delivery to ethnic people. Development of alternative service delivery models applicable to the minorities is crucial to increasing services utilization among the underserved. Neighborhood based support systems should build on the strengths of the helping networks that operate in neighborhoods. A framework built on five A's is offered for consideration to ensure quality of services. These include: Accessibility, Availability, Acceptability, Appropriateness, and Accountability. The use of the five A's will provide necessary data to reward effective and efficient program performers and deny the funding of programs that consistently fail to achieve acceptable standards of performance.

228. Rathbone-McCuan, E. E., Hooyman, N., and Fortune, A. E. (1985). Social support for the frail elderly. In Sauer, W. J. and Coward, R. T. (Eds.). Social Support Networks and the Care of the Elderly. New York: Springer Publishing Company, 234-247.

The focus of this chapter is on the frail elderly, defined as those persons who may be institutionalized (or are at risk of institutionalization) but who could, with some assistance, be maintained in the community. Four conditions of mental and physical impairments combine to make an elderly person frail and in need for support from their social networks: 1) unsafe without significant and regular assistance from others; 2) unstable with rapid and unpredictable functional setbacks; 3) not reversible to any significant extent because of chronic conditions, and 4) unmanageable in the community without some extensive support from informal, nonpaid sources. There are no clear policies with respect to sharing responsibility for the frail elderly between the formal and informal support systems. Nor are there adequate data for policy formulation. The impact of care giving on both giver and receiver needs to be explored as well.

229. Roberto, K. A., and Scott, J. P. (1984-85). Friendship patterns among older women, International Journal of Aging and Human Development, 19(1):1-10.

The importance of friendship in the lives of older women was highlighted in a study which examined 105 white, middle-class, urban women, aged 65 and older. Results indicated that widowed women received more help from their friends than did married women. Those who benefitted equitably from their friendships and women who gave more help than they received had a higher mean morale score than did women who received more help than they gave. Implications of these findings for friendship support systems in late life are presented.

230. Shulik, R. N. Faith development, moral development, and old age: An assessment of Fowler's faith development paradigm. Doctoral dissertation, The University of Chicago, 1979. Dissertation Abstracts International, 40(6-B):2907.

Fowler's theory of faith development parallels that of moral development postulated by Kohlberg. Fowler has also developed an empirical methodology to assess subjects' faith-stage levels. This methodology was utilized with forty subjects between the ages of 56 and 86. Findings indicated that faith development stage is significantly related to the respondent's subjective awareness of changes occuring with old age. Almost none of the subjects were engaged in deliberate processes of life-review or preparations for death. It was concluded that the various structural-developmental theories are describing different facets of a common developmental process.

231. Shwayder-Hughes, M. L. The impact of institutionalization upon the Jewish aged: A comparative approach, Doctoral dissertation, University of Colorado at Boulder, 1979. Dissertation Abstracts International, 40(4): 2298-A, Order No. 7923286.

Using a symbolic interactionist perspective, this study compared 36 residents in an apartment complex for the aged with 36 residents in a home for the aged. A scale of anomie and alienation was derived by utilizing factor analysis. Institutionalization was found to be related to the age of the individual and to his/her child's upward mobility. Socially induced problems are expressed in a sense of alienation among institutionalized elderly. Being a member of a stigmatized group in a social setting that infantilizes the aged is detrimental to the mental health of the aging. Alteration of the social conditions, such as encouragement of independence, will allow individuals to reject stigmatization and will improve their self-concept.

232. Snyder, P. (1982). Creating culturally supportive environments in long-term care institutions. Journal of Long Term Care
Administration, 10(1):19-28.

Long term care institutions have distinctive features and fairly
regimented activities encompassing all of one's daily life. Conformity with numerous federal certification and state licensure
requirements impose specific standards and limitations both on the
physical environment and on the social environment. Attempts to
promote a more home-like environment may fail when the cultural
component of these environments are neglected, and when cultural
preferences of the residents are not taken into account in programming. Administration and staff should be sensitive to the
cultural heritages of the residents and to their preferences in
food, activities, celebration of holidays and special needs.

233. Steinitz, L. Y. (1984). Psychosocial effects of the Holocaust on aging survivors and their families. Journal of Jewish
Communal Service, 60(4):331-336.

Survivors of the Holocaust are largely aged by now. These
people consist of a special category for whom the conventional
judgments of clinicians of "good" or "bad" psychosocial adjustment
do not apply. In this exploratory study conducted with aging
survivors, with their children, and with 40 clinicians and researchers associated with the Group Project for Holocaust Survivors and their children, the unique reactions of the survivors to
the residual effects of the War's trauma were investigated.
Issues of intergenerational communication, loss, long-term care
for the frail parent, and positive coping capacities are described, and several treatment, program, and research implications are
raised.

234. Suziedelis, G. (1980). Response of Galina Suziedelis. In
Civil Rights Issues of Euro-Ethnic Americans in the United States:
Opportunities and Challenges. Washington, D. C.: U. S. Govern-
ment Printing Office, No. 629843/6080, 360-363.

"To be female even in today's society is still often a mixed
blessing at best; but research shows that to allow oneself to
become an aged female immigrant is not only risky, but downright a
mistake." This statement of the author is supported by findings
from a study on eight ethnic groups in the Baltimore-Washington,
D. C. area (Guttmann, et al., 1979) in which respondents of Lithuanian, Latvian, Estonian, Hungarian, Polish, Italian, Greek, and
Jewish-American background differed significantly by sex. There
were more women than men with low education, more women living
alone, more widows, more in poverty and more with a low degree of
life satisfaction. Their self-image was shaped by their achievements in the area of family and child bearing. Those without
children tended to view themselves as failures. The needs of

elderly ethnic women from all social classes are similar. They
want to be in a familiar place and do what is culturally meaningful to them. They need warmth, especially by caretakers when they
are frail, and this includes the ability to communicate in the
ethnic language of childhood, which they retain and revert to as
they near death. These needs must be understood and respected by
those who work with ethnic women in nursing homes.

235. Szekais, B. (1985). Risk factors for institutionalization in
a community elderly population. Physical and Occupational Therapy
in Geriatrics, 4(1):33-43.

The prevention of premature institutionalization of the aged is
a formidable task. It is usually assumed that as an age group,
the elderly are at a higher risk than the young for institutionalization. Factors which might result in higher risk of institutionalization were investigated with 50 adult day care center
clients. Approximately half of this group had been institutionalized at least once in the year prior to enrollment in the day
care center. Their data were compared with those of the sample
who were not previously institutionalized. Results indicated no
significant differences between the two groups, highlighting the
lack of predictive factors. The task to further investigate and
identify elderly at risk of institutionalization is stressed.

236. Vinick, B. H. (1984). Elderly men as caretakers of wives.
Journal of Geriatric Psychiatry, 17(1):61-66.

Widows outnumber widowers by a ratio of one to six. Older men
tend to marry younger women, while the latter outlive men by an
average of eight years. Most research on caretaking of disabled
and frail older people has focused on elderly wives taking care of
their spouses, and on children, especially middle-aged daughters,
caring for an elderly parent. Yet, there are many men who carry
on caretaking functions of their spouses.
This study, while not representative and based on a small non-
probability sample, is calling attention to this neglected aspect
in research on caretaking. The 25 widowers in the sample took
primary responsibility for caregiving, which ranged from minor
assistance for relatively intact spouses to feeding, toileting and
turning over in the bed completely dependent wives. The strain
among these caregivers was significantly related to negative
attitudes toward remarriage. The need for respite services and
opportunities to share experiences and feelings for these men, and
more research on the role of men as caregivers are stressed.

237. Wish, F. (1980). Day care: Its value for the older adult
and his family. Journal of Jewish Communal Service, 57(2):174-
180.

Day care services to older adults were initially developed in
the 1940s by psychiatric day hospitals. Today there are three
distinct types or day care centers: 1) thos⌐ in senior centers
that deal primarily with persons who are in relatively good
health; 2) those that provide a protective environment to persons
with limited functional capacity, and 3) day care centers for the
severely handicapped, who need health care, rehabilitation services and support. An emerging day care program is geared to the
mentally impaired elderly. Common to all types of day care centers for older adults is that they emphasize social and health
programming. These services benefit the elderly and their families.

238. Zoot, V. A. (1980). A program to reduce spiritual depriva-
tion in the nursing home. In Thorson, J. A. and Cook, T. C., Jr.
(Eds.). Spiritual Well-being of the Elderly. Springfield, Ill:
Charles C. Thomas, 195-197.

A Jewish congregation in Skokie, Illinois began a program of
weekly services and celebrations of holidays in 1976. The residents in the facility were quite pleased, especially those among
them who were Jewish. Religious congregations can be effective in
bringing about positive change in long term care.

5
Current Research about Euro-American Elderly

Studies of Specific Ethnic Groups

239. Cadigan, D. A. Health care utilization by the elderly: An application of the Andersen Model. Doctoral dissertation, The Johns Hopkins University, 1984. Dissertation Abstracts International, 45(11):3458-A, Order No. DA8501625.

Illness level, enabling and predisposing factors used in the Andersen model to predict outpatient and hospital utilization for a sample of 274 Jewish elderly were studied. All three groups of factors were significant predictors of health care utilization. Respondents with more education were more likely to have visited a physician. Being a member of a religious congregation, and being unmarried, significantly predicted the volume of physician visits, while age was inversely related to use. In this sample the Andersen model did not predict hospitalization well. An implication of these findings is that health service utilization should be considered only one of a number of possible responses to physical symptoms.

240. Flynn, J. Z. Dress of Older Italian-American women: Documentation of dress and the influence of socio-cultural factors. Doctoral dissertation, The Ohio State University, 1979. Dissertation Abstracts International, 40:4238-A. Order No. 8001728.

Based on field research, changes in dress of older Italian-American women moving from a rural to an urban society are investigated in the context of socio-cultural factors affecting their lives. Dress was viewed in relation to a continuum with three features of change selected to be analyzed: (1) the movement from family life to individuality; (2) the movement from neighborhood to city; and (3) the movement from religion to rationalities.

241. Gerrity, P. L. By ourselves: An ethnographic study of self-care in an elderly Jewish population. Doctoral dissertation, University of Pennsylvania, 1983. Dissertation Abstracts International, 44(07):2244-A, Order No. DA 8326292.

Self care is defined as an initiative which individuals take on their own behalf with the specific expectation of health promotion and for the prevention and treatment of disease. Using an ethnographic approach, elderly Russian-Jewish former small business owners were interviewed. These people relocated from the inner city to an outlying urban neighborhood with the hope of spending there the remainder of their lives. Self-care was found to constitute a large portion of activity, and was based on deeply rooted cultural beliefs and shared peer experiences. The common background and values served as guide to their responses to pain and helped to provide content and purpose to their lives.

242. Johnson, E. S. (1981-82). Role expectations and role realities of older Italian mothers and their daughters. International Journal of Aging and Human Development, 14(4):271-276.

Ninety pairs of older unmarried Italian American women and their daughters comprised a sample for studying their role expectations and realities in Boston, Massachusetts. Giving advice, providing emotional support, participating in household activities, and being generally available to one another were areas in which there was a relatively high level of consensus between mothers in terms of mutual expectations. Daughters desired less advice and more emotional support from their mothers, while the latter exhibited more role confusion about what they felt their children should expect and what they could provide. Level of anxiety in mother child relationships was tied to ability to fulfill desires.

243. Moore, D. D. The emergence of ethnicity: New York's Jews, 1920-1940. Doctoral dissertation, Columbia University, 1975. Dissertation Abstracts International, 36(12-A):8255.

Children of the immigrants, or the second generation, raised the question of the nature of group assimilation into American society rather vividly. Acculturation, accompanied by ethnic group persistence, was the answer. In New York City between 1920 and 1940 second generation Jews accomodated themselves to American life while they fashioned social and cultural institutions to promote Jewish ethnic group separateness.

244. Smith, J. E. (1978). Our own kind: Family and community networks. Radical History Review, 17:99-120.

The experience of the urban industrial environment of Rhode Island in a period of 60 years, from 1880 through 1940, is reviewed. The study encompasses southern Italian and eastern European Jewish immigrants, their family ties and traditions, and the importance of the community networks for their well-being.

245. Wright, B. Self–help among the elderly, a study of exchange in two social activity centers. Doctoral dissertation, Columbia University, 1984. Dissertation Abstracts International,45(10): 3213–A, Order No. DA8427498.

Data collected in face–to face interviews with 48 elderly Jewish females between the ages of 71 and 75 years were analyzed. Subjects' involvement in self–help activities and their use of services from social service agencies indicated that the older members had no spouses and were more likely to engage in exchange activities with their children than did younger subjects. Social service agencies were sought out to provide help with paying major medical bills, for making household repairs, and for extended skill nursing care. Greater collaboration between the formal and the informal service delivery systems is advocated, as both are needed for effective assistance to the needy elderly.

Comparative Studies

246. Berrol, S. C. (1976). School days on the old east side: The Italian and Jewish experience. New York History, 57(2):201–213.

Many of the present generation of elderly Italian and Jewish Americans grew up on the east side of New York City. Their school day experiences in the early decades of the 1900's are compared. These immigrants from the Old World brought with them their traditional attitudes toward education which explain the differences between the two ethnic groups with respect to academic success. Jewish children in general were taught by their parents to look upon education as the key to success, while Italians were more leery of the school's place in reaching the same goal. Only in later generations, with the growing Americanization of the Italians, were the academic performances of these two groups more equal.

247. Cantor, M. H. (1979). Effect of ethnicity on life styles of the inner–city elderly. In Hendricks J. and Hendricks, C.D.(Eds.). Dimensions of Aging: Readings, Cambridge, Massachusetts: Winthrop Publishers, Inc. 278–293.

In 1970 the New–York City Office for the Aging undertook one of the first and most comprehensive cross–cultural studies of the urban elderly poor living in the inner city. A sample of 1,552 respondents, sixty years old and older and non–institutionalized elderly, representing the three major ethnic groups in the city, comprised 49 percent white, 37 percent black and 13 percent Spanish speaking elderly (principally of Puerto Rican origin). The purpose of the study was to learn about the lifestyles and the support systems used by these people and their need for assistance. Findings revealed that the health of the inner–city elderly is poorer than older people generally. The majority of the sample lived in dismal economic and social conditions, with incomes abysmally low, significantly below the city wide levels for older people. Ethnic differences among the respondents were noted in median income, in employment and work history, and in retirement pensions, with white elderly having significantly higher levels in each of these categories than either blacks or Hispanics. Despite their poverty, elderly ethnics assisted their children at similar levels in all three groups in times of crisis and with chores of daily living. In turn, over 67 percent of the children helped the parents in time of illness. These strengths and difficulties need to be taken into consideration in planning services for these elderly.

248. Cohler, B. J. and Leiberman, M. A. (1979). Personality change across the second half of life: Findings from a study of Irish, Italian, and Polish-American men and women. In Gelfand, D. E. and Kutzik, A. J. (Eds.). Ethnicity and Aging, Theory, Research and Policy. New York: Springer Publishing Company, 227-245.

This chapter discusses the impact of ethnicity in shaping the course of personality change across the second half of life. The extent to which ethnicity influences the expression of achievement, perception of locus of control over environment and self, and characteristic masculine and feminine preferences were compared between middle-aged and older men and women within each ethnic group. A total of 386 men and women, 40 to 80 years of age, either first or second generation Irish, Italian, or Polish respondents in Chicago were interviewed. Concern with achievement was found to be the single most powerful factor differentiating between the middle aged and the older group. There is some confirmation for a theory of personality change across the second half of life, while ethnicity appears to have an impact upon the process of this change.

249. Fandetti, D. V. and Gelfand, D. E. (1978). Attitudes toward symptoms and services in the ethnic family and neighborhood. American Journal of Orthopsychiatry, 48 (3):477-486.

The extended family in Italian and Polish neighborhoods in Baltimore, Maryland, is seen as the "first line of defense" and as resource for initial advice on emotional problems. Mental health specialists on the other hand are seldom perceived as appropriate agents for meeting problems that are beyond the expertise of the family. The importance of certain individuals in the local community as providers of intensive assistance is emphasized, and implications for community mental health are examined.

250. Guttmann, D. (1979). Use of informal and formal supports by white ethnic aged. In Gelfand, D. E. and Kutzik, A. J. (Eds.). Ethnicity and Aging, Theory, Research and Policy. New York: Springer Publishing Company, 246-262.

Eight white ethnic groups of elderly and their spokespersons were studied in Washington, D.C. and Baltimore Maryland. The sample comprised of 720 elderly and 180 non-elderly ethnics representing the Estonian, Latvian, Lithuanian, Polish, Hungarian, Jewish, Italian, and Greek communities. The symbolic interaction theory served as the conceptual basis for this research. Attention was focused on the problems and needs of ethnic elderly and on their use of services, both formal and informal, as well as on their reliance on the ethnic community for support. Findings reveal little use of formal services, and raise questions as to the effectiveness of the programs available to the ethnic aged. Theoretical and practical implications of the findings are offered.

251. Huber, L. W. (1985). Connections: A study of the place of the church in the personal networks of the aged. Social Work Research and Abstracts, 21(3), 48.

Using network analysis techniques, a random sample of aged members of an Episcopal church, a black Baptist church, and a Polish Roman Catholic church were interviewed to determine their personal networks and the place the church holds in them. Significant differences emerged among the churches in relation to the extent and type of involvement they had in the networks of elderly church members. Changes in the importance of the church over the course of the lifetimes of their members are noted, and tentative guidelines offered to aid practitioners in working with aged individuals through the church.

252. Johnson, E. S. (1978). "Good" relationships between older mothers and their daughters: A causal model. The Gerontologist, 18(3):301-306.

Four life areas: health, finances, living arrangement, and attitudes toward aging, were examined as they influence the affective quality of the adult child-elderly parent relationships. Subjects were 90 pairs of single Italian-American mothers, 60 years of age or over, and their adult daughters, selected from a non-institutionalized population. Factor and path analysis were used to analyze the data. Only living arrangement and attitude toward aging had large direct effects on family relationships. Policy implications of these findings are presented.

253. Kahana, E. and Felton, B. J. (1977). Social context and personal need: A study of Polish and Jewish aged. Journal of Social Issues, 33(4): 56-74.

Interviews conducted with a sample of 402 older people living in a predominantly Polish or Jewish neighborhood with respect to their service needs reveal similarities despite their cultural and life-style differences. These needs are most acute in the areas

of housing, health care, and finances. The problems facing researchers in studying ethnic aged are also reviewed.

Among these are instrumentation, access, and interpretation of
the data. There are ethical issues as well, such as studying disadvantaged elderly without providing for their needs.

254. Kessner, T. The golden door: Immigrant mobility in New York
City, 1880-1915. Doctoral dissertation, Columbia University,
1975. Dissertation Abstracts International, 36:3071-A.

Between 1880 and 1915 New York City attracted a very large number of immigrants. The newcomers differed from those others who
preceded them because of their non-Protestant religion and their
peasant folkways. These impoverished immigrants from south Italy
and East Europe settled in New York's downtown neighborhoods.
They also caused much concern among the nativists who feared that
they would not be able to adjust to life in a big city. History
proved these fears not particularly realistic, as Italians and
Jews serve a good example of social mobility in America.

255. Krause, C. A. (1978). Urbanization without breakdown: Italian, Jewish, and Slavic immigrant women in Pittsburgh, 1900-1945.
Journal of Urban History, 4(3):291-306.

Oral histories taken from immigrant Italian, Slavic, and Jewish
women reveal their resiliency in meeting the cultural shock of immigration to the New World. These women used ethnic neighborhood
organizations and their cultural bridges to the old world as bul-
warks against mental breakdown. Their adjustment to life in America without a serious or lasting problem can serve as an example
to present and future generations of immigrant women.

256. Krause, C. A. (1982). Grandmothers, Mothers and Daughters An
Oral History Study of Ethnicity, Mental Health, and Continuity of
Three Generations of Jewish, Italian, and Slavic-American Women.
American Jewish Committee, New York.

Offering a close look at three generations of ethnic women who
live in the industrial Northeast, this study was undertaken to
identify information about ethnic women and ethnicity as expressed
and perceived by them that may be useful to educators, scholars
and to professionals responsible for the delivery of mental health
services. Retention of the ethnic identity is a central factor in
the lives of these women. Despite some weakening of the informal
supports, that traditionally were the major sources of good mental
health, these are still extending their influence over the well-
being of ethnic women. Identification of generational and ethnic
differences in priorities, interests, and problems can help us
recognize potential areas of conflict. It can also serve as a
basis for the perception of common interests, values and goals,

and may lead to coalition building for facing the challenges of
modern society.   These were the conclusions reached from this
study of 225 women in Pittsburgh equally divided among three generations of three major ethnic groups.

257. Lareau, L. S. and Heumann, L. F. (1982).   The inadequacy of
needs assessments of the elderly.   The Gerontologist, 22(3):324-
330.

Needs assessment of the elderly have become standard procedures
by state and local governments over the past decade.   They serve
evidence when arguing for federal support, for planning requirements, and for entitlement grants.   They are also used by private
agencies to show private investors where needs exist and to seek
contribution from foundations and from charitable organizations.
Despite their widespread use, little is known about the quality of
needs assessment.   This study presents the findings from an evaluation of needs assessments produced by agencies involved in planning services for the elderly.   A total of 400 agencies was included in the survey, and 252 or 63% responded.   Major flaws in
the documents presented by these agencies included inappropriate
methods of quantifying needs, repeated patterns of over or under
counting, and use of indicators inappropriate to the needs or
services being studied.
Several conclusions were reached by the researchers; 1) more
care must be taken with research methods, 2) deficiencies in the
descriptive variables need to be overcome, and 3) descriptive
variables should include household size and relationships of
household members, sex, age, income, health or functional ability
levels, and housing tenure.   The states with the support of the
federal government must become the initial sources for improving
regional planning agency needs assessment of the elderly.

258. Mostwin, D. (1979).   Emotional needs of elderly Americans of
central and eastern European background.   In D. E. Gelfand and A.
J. Kutzik (Eds.).   Ethnicity and Aging: Theory, Research, and
Policy.   New York: Springer Publishing Company, 263-276.

The need for love, which for the elderly means care and respect;
the need for survival, expressed in the wish to be part of a
whole, and the need for creativity, meaning self expression, indi-
viduation and striving for self-sufficiency are studied in the
life space of a sample consisting of 160 elderly Poles from Washington, D.C. and Baltimore. Another large sample of 2,845 elderly
Poles in Poland serve as comparison.   This chapter is based on a
large study involving 900 subjects from eight different ethnic
communities.   The findings imply the importance of family ties and
milieu for fulfillment of the need for love.   Each group considers
its own culture as worthy of preservation and transmission to the
younger generation.   Hence the need for survival as the continua-
tion of cultural heritage.   Creativity is expressed in ethnic
crafts and in visiting others, or attending church services.

These activities require a sharing of oneself with another person. Ethnic institutions promote a sense of well-being and self-actualization and enhance the emotional health of the elderly.

259. Shandler, M. A. A study of the attitudes toward psychotherapy of American German Jews and selected groups of American East European Jews. Doctoral dissertation, The Catholic University of America, 1979. Studies in Social Work, No. 131. Dissertation Abstracts International, 40(2):1078-1079-A, Order No, 7918580.

In this comparative study a sample of 60 German and 60 East European adult Jews was interviewed. Both groups are Ashkenazic Jews, yet each group has a discrete identity. German Jews are known to have come from a more urban, affluent, entrepreneurial, assimilationist, and religiously liberal background. East European Jews, by contrast, came from a more rural, laboring, clannish, and religiously orthodox background. These characteristics of the two groups were assumed to affect their attitudes toward psychotherapy.

Findings indicated that the German Jews had statistically more significant positive attitude toward psychotherapy than did the East European Jews. Prior experience with psychotherapy is independent of a person's background, Jewish identity, or religious affiliation. The author concludes that different ethnic groups possess culturally determined attitudes toward social institutions and services, and that these differ with each ethnic group. Social workers are urged to incorporate such knowledge into their services delivery system.

Multi-Ethnic Studies

260. Getzel, G. S. (1982). Helping elderly couples in crisis. Social Casework, 63(9):515-521.

Marital bonding and spousal caregiving are significant resources in old age. However, chronic impairment and illness often place heavy demands on elderly spouses in meeting caregiving expectations and day-to-day needs. The Natural Support Program (NSP), developed by the Community Service Society of New York City, is aimed at exploring the value of providing an innovative service, including a range of social services and cash benefits, to caregivers for elderly relatives in the community. The impact of the caregiving function on the marital relationship of older couples is illustrated with case descriptions and analysis.

261. Gitelman, P. J. Morale, self-concept, and social integration: A comparative study of Black and Jewish aged, urban poor. Doctoral dissertation, Rutgers University, The State University of New Jersey, 1976. Dissertation Abstracts International, 37(6-A): 3907-3908.

Racial, ethnic, and religious differences, although significant, are not sufficient in and of themselves to account for aging individuals' self-appraisal and morale. Two distinct groups of aged urban poor Blacks and Jews formed the study population. Adjustment to old age was measured by three dependent variables, each subdivided into four dimensions: morale, self-concept and social integration. Married Blacks generally scored high on all dimensions, as anticipated, while married Jewish females scored the lowest. Findings confirmed the impact of religion, race and ethnicity on adjustment to old age. Implications for policy planning and service delivery are presented along with ideas for future research.

262. Guttmann, D. (1978).   Life events and decision making by older adults. The Gerontologist, 18(5):462–467.

Decision making related to life events was studied in an exploratory study with 410 elderly subjects representing the larger population of the elderly in terms of age, sex, marital status, income and race, in the Washington, D.C. Standard Metropolitan Statistical Area. Age, education, income, and satisfaction with decisions made were the significant variables in perceiving life events as positive or negative, while action taking was strongly associated with well-being in old age. Implications of these findings for the self-perception of the elderly are discussed as a relevant research area for social gerontology.

263. Hunt, T. C. (1976).   The schooling of immigrants and Black Americans: Some similarities and differences. Journal of Negro Education, 45(4):423–431.

Can education offset a long history of oppression and frustration and lead to upward mobility? It cannot, says the author of this article. Black children who migrated to northern cities during 1940–1966, and immigrant children from southern and eastern Europe, who came to the United States between 1890 and 1920, differ from each other in their motivation for success. The former were not upwardly mobile, unlike the latter, because they did not come to this country willingly to better their future and because of the oppression they had to experience and endure.

264. Johnson, E. S. (1983). Suburban older women. In Markson, E. W. (Ed.). Older Women, D.C. Heath and Company, Lexington, Massachusetts, 179–193.

The author presents the story (and a brief history) of thirty nine elderly women of different ethnic and racial backgrounds, among them married, widowed, and never married women, all of them 65 years old and older, who live in one of the suburbs of Boston, Massachusetts. Common to all these women is that they lived in the same community but did not belong to any organization, nor did they receive services from particular agencies. These women may be seen to some extent as the representatives of a growing suburban population of elderly, of whom not much is known at the present. As a group, these women characterize the great variety found among the elderly in general. They vary in their housing and living arrangements, in their expectations from life, in their reliance on their children in case of need, and in their life satisfactions. For women without spouses or children, relationships with siblings and friends were particularly significant, as expected. This study reaffirms the theory of continuity in aging, which explains the importance of accustumed ways of life during the previous phases of the life cycle as indicative of the way people deal with the changes in their lives in old age.

265. Johnson, L. M. Religious patterns, coping mechanisms, and life satisfaction of the Black and White aged. Doctoral dissertation, Saint Louis University, 1978. Dissertation Abstracts International, 39(10-A):6337, Order No. 7908284.

This dissertation is an exploratory study of the religious patterns manifested by the black and white aged and the impact of religious involvement on increased life satisfaction. Religion and church functions were assumed to offer social outlets and an escape from an intolerable life more for the black than the white aged. The hypotheses that black aged would manifest higher levels of religiosity and greater use of religion as an adaptive mechanism to cope with strains were confirmed. Both black and white aged in the sample had similar levels of life satisfaction, but high levels of religiosity were not associated with high levels of life satisfaction.

266. McCaslin, R. and Calvert, W. R. (1975). Social indicators in black and white: Some ethnic considerations in delivery of service to the elderly. Journal of Gerontology, 30 (1):60-66.

This research was aimed at "teasing out" working hypotheses regarding the effect of client ethnicity on the presentation of need at the threshold of the service delivery system. Subjects were a sample of older persons who contacted the information service for the aged in Houston. Data obtained through the central intake office were compared with data from an independent citywide sample to which the same instrument was administered. Significant differences were found in the sample obtained through the central intake - referral service on measures of income, health and life satisfaction. Differences found between the two samples were combined to provide indications of cultural factors involved in services utilization by the elderly. The need to consider ethnic differences in designing services to the aging and in the development of theories on aging is discussed.

267. Silverstein, N. M. (1984). Informing the elderly about public services: The relationship between sources of knowledge and service utilization. The Gerontologist, 24(1):37-40.

Many elderly people need health and welfare services, but paradoxically, many elderly underutilize available resources, or use them selectively. The critical role of information in service use was examined with 706 men and women 60 years of age and over in Boston. Subjects were selected by systematic probability sampling and included the major ethnic groups in the city according to their proportions in the total elderly population of the nation. Knowledge of services depends on the source of information. Generally, most respondents learned of services through the media or through informal sources. Implications of these findings for information - referral services, outreach, and inclusion of the informal network in dissemination of knowledge about services are discussed.

6
Education and Training
for Working with
Euro-American Elderly

Theories of Ethnicity and Aging

268. Banks, J. A. and Gay, G. (1978). Ethnicity in contemporary American society: Toward the development of a typology. Ethnicity, 5(3):238-251.

A new definition of an ethnic group is offered to underline the changes in the study of ethnicity that have occured in the past two decades. According to this definition, an ethnic group is an involuntary group whose members share a sense of peoplehood and an interdependence of fate. Notions of a common religious or common geographic or national bond are absent from this definition. The emphasis instead is on culture, economics, or political themes around which various types of ethnic groups cluster and on the interrelationships between ethnic identification, ethnic heritage and culture. The prevailing social, economic, and political conditions influence the degree of ethnicity.

269. Baum, M. and Baum, R. C. (1982). Psycho-moral health in the later years: Some network correlates. In Biegel, D. E. and Naparstek (Eds.). Community Support Systems and Mental Health Practice, Policy and Research. New York: Springer Publishing Company, 54-72.

Positive psycho-moral health in later life was postulated as being the joint function of: 1) the ability to reduce the scope of reasonable alternatives against which the worth of one's life is measured; 2) the ability to reduce personal responsibility for the actual life one has lived; and 3) receiving aid in these two tasks through status homophily in social affiliations and identifications with one's intimates in old age. These three mechanisms provide a sense of meaning and embeddedness in social subgroups, which in turn can shield persons from some of the alienating aspects of our society. Erikson's concept of integrity in old age as the desired outcome of development in human behavior served as the theoretical basis for this study with 106 subjects from four ethnic groups in Pittsburg. Chronological age was set at seventy to reduce the effect of age as a variable. Results indicated that social homophily, or being embedded in a close circle of intimates "of one's own kind," has the most potent positive influence on well-being, whether it operates through ethnicity, religion or social class. Some implications of these findings for practice are presented.

270. Bengtson, V. L. (1979). Ethnicity and aging: Problems and issues in current social science inquiry. In D. E. Gelfand and A. J. Kutzik (Eds.), Ethnicity and Aging: Theory, Research, and Policy. New York: Springer Publishing Company, 9-31.

Several problems recurrently faced by social scientists in research on ethnicity and aging are summarized as consisting of the lack of systematic information which spans both research and policy. Data from the University of Southern California's community survey of aging and social policy, involving 1,269 individuals from Black, Mexican-American, and white communities were analyzed on four dimensions reflecting quality of life: income, health, social interaction, and life satisfaction. The white ethnics were not differentiated as to their cultural backgrounds. Significant differences among these ethnic groups were noted with respect to the four dimensions cited. Age exerts a leveling influence on ethnic variation.

271. Biegel, D. E. (1985). The application of network theory and research to the field of aging. In Sauer, W. J. and Coward, R. T. (Eds.). Social Support Networks and the Care of the Elderly. New York: Springer Publishing Company, 251-273.

This chapter summarizes the state of the art in research about social support systems and their utilization by the elderly. Issues related to the strengths, weaknesses, and limitations of these systems are discussed using social network theory and research as the conceptual framework for this discussion. Also cited are models of social network intervention, and obstacles, limitations, and/or difficulties in developing interventions. Professionals can provide assistance to family caretakers of the elderly in taking advantage of the many educational and training programs aimed at enhancing their skills, knowledge and understanding of the aging process. Family care-givers may be encouraged to join groups for mutual support and assistance. The need for assessing the value of the intervention and the quality of the relationship and informal services is stressed.

272. Cook, J. W. An application of the disengagement theory of aging to older persons in the church. Doctoral dissertation, Boston University School of Theology, 1971. Dissertation Abstracts International, 33(6-A):3011.

The purpose of this study was to discover whether older persons, white Roman Catholics and Protestants from several denominations who retire and move to Florida, disengage from the church more than those who remain in their home community. The 95 subjects in the sample were of similar backgrounds. Findings supported the disengagement theory of aging. There was a decrease in church attendance. Piety did not increase with age. Implications of this study for the church are discussed and a series of recommendations on what to do is offered. The final conclusion states that activity is not the panacea for all problems of aging. Not all older adults want to be kept busy. Some are happy to disengage from the pressures of middle age.

273. Dashefsky, A. (1975). Theoretical frameworks in the study of ethnic identity: Toward a social psychology of ethnicity. Ethnicity, 2(1):10-18.

Studies on ethnic identity have been focused largely on Afro-Americans and Jewish-Americans, while various Euro-American ethnic groups were mostly forgotten. There is still much confusion about the concept of ethnic identity, due largely to a lack of sufficient theoretical integration.

This paper offers four theoretical frameworks as points of departure in studying ethnic identity: sociocultural, interactionist, group dynamicist, and psychoanalytic. For each of these frameworks the major assumptions and derived propositions are set forth and an illustrative example using Erikson's concept of identity, is discussed.

274. Greeley, A. M. (1973). What is an ethnic? In Ryan, J. (Ed.). White Ethnics: Their Life in Working-Class America. Englewood Cliffs, New Jersey: Prentice-Hall, 11-16.

Frequent changes in the population make definitions of ethnicity and ethnic groups quickly obsolete. Many of the elements of ethnicity cannot be defined. Ethnicity is composed largely of a feeling, of belonging emotionally to a group whose members one feels are connected to him or her by virtue of a common ancestry, history, geography, religion, and/or kinship. The survival of the ethnic group is made possible in America due to the tolerance, both cultural and religious, of the founding fathers and mothers toward the immigrants - despite their different national origin or religion. The importance of being an ethnic is explained by the author as based on an intimate relationship between ethnicity and religion. A primordial feeling of belongingness to a distinct group enhances this perception. There is a distinction between "we" and "they" irrespective of logic and reality. Such feelings persist even in the face of irrefutable realities. Diversity in cultures and in religions can foster distrust, prejudice, and strife. It can also be an enriching factor for the larger society, especially when irrational fears are eliminated and when mutual respect is fostered among the diverse ethnic groups.

275. Hayes, C. L., Giordano, J. and Levine, I. M. (1986).   The
need for education and training.   In Hayes, C. L., Kalish, R. A.
and Guttmann, D. (Eds.).   European-American Elderly: A Guide for
Practice. New York: Springer Publishing Company, 212-229.

During the last decade much progress has been made to train service providers in working with the aged.   Much of the training focused on the generally recognized minority aged, such as Black,
Hispanic, Asian/Pacific and Native-American elderly.   Although the
1981 White House Mini-Conference on Euro-American elderly strongly
recommended increased training for service providers and religious
personnel to serve this segment of the aged population, so far
little progress has been made.   A multi-ethnic perspective in
training gerontologists and other services providers is needed to
adress the needs of the many diverse ethnic groups in American society.
   The role of various agencies and institutions in training present and future service providers in explicated.   Attention should
focus on basic principles, problems, resources and strategies that
services providers will have to address in their work with ethnic
elderly.   Broadening of the service providers' cultural world-
views; enhancing relevant skills; addressing client resistance;
dealing with the larger social system, and focusing on the
strength of the ethnic community are advocated.

276. Holzberg, C. S. (1982).   Ethnicity and aging: Anthropological
perspectives on more than just the minority elderly.   The Gerontologist, 22(3):249-257.

Most of the research on the ethnic elderly tended to concentrate
on deprived minorities.   As a consequence ethnicity has been mud-
dled. The relevance of ethnicity to psycho-social adjustment in
aging and the importance of the cultural dimension for gerontological research are explicated.   Differentiation of the cultural
heritages of ethnic groups is necessary for an enlightened services provision, as these explain why certain people behave as well
as age differently from others.   Problems with the focus on "minority" literature include superficial attention to the effects of
differentiated cultural styles in the aging process, and treating
various ethnic population segments as if they were culturally
homogeneous.   Research that treats ethnicity as a significant independent variable can only result in the improvement of service
delivery to the elderly population as a whole.

277. Holzberg, C. S. (1982).   Ethnicity and aging: Rejoinder to a
Comment by Kyriakos S. Markides." The Gerontologist, 22 (6):471-
472.

Holzberg found it necessary to reply to the comment raised by
Markides stating that: 1) culture has been overlooked because it
is not perceived as a significant determinant of behavior, and 2)

that it is often not distinguished from the effects of social class and racial discrimination. Ethnic and cultural differences in aging do exist and these must be taken into consideration in policy-making and in services delivery. Availability of funds for research on white ethnics, or their lack from the government, should not deter gerontologists from focusing their research efforts on these groups, as well as on other minorities, and can raise the level of sensitivity and awareness about both.

278. Isaacs, H. R. (1974). Basic group identity: The idols of the tribe. Ethnicity, 1(1):15-41.

Endowments and identifications acquired by birth, or at the time of birth, represent man's essential tribalism. Rooted in the need for security, belonging, and self-esteem, this essential tribalism provides the individual with a sense of basic group identity. Included in this concept are such personal characteristics as name, status, language and religion, as well as physical attributes. The works of Sigmund Freud, Erik Erikson, and Erich Fromm are cited as the sources for the ideas pertaining to the notion of what constitutes basic group identity and its manifestation in human behavior.

279. Kastenbaum, R. (1979). Reflections on old age, ethnicity and death. In Gelfand, D. E. and Kutzik, A. J. (Eds.). Ethnicity and Aging, Theory, Research, and Practice, New York: Springer Publishing Company, 81-95.

The changing importance ethnicity might have for individuals at different times of their lives is discussed in this article. The author raises questions based on his experience as a psychologist and sets forth problems and possibilities that could make it easier for clinicians, researchers, administrators, and educators to fathom the interrelationships of death, aging, and ethnicity. Separating ethnicity as though it were a static variable does violence to the dynamic integrity of the individual. Awareness of ethnic values held dear by old people is not only necessary for health care providers. It is equally important for the individual for whom the care is provided, for it may enable them to take pride in being what themselves.

280. Katlin, F. (1982). The impact of ethnicity. Social Casework, 63(3):168-171.

Ethnic values affecting Jewish clients were blended with clinical social work in seminars for staff working in a Jewish agency with clients of similar religio-ethnic backgrounds. Participants shared memories, feelings, and experiences, and came to appreciate the importance of ethnic identity for both worker and client. Understanding the components of ethnic identity and of ethnic bonding are considered therapeutic tools for diagnosis and treatment.

Social workers are urged to view ethnicity as a major factor in one's adaptation to life.

281. Kutzik, A. J. (1979). American social provision for the aged: An historical perspective. In Gelfand, D. E. and Kutzik, A. J. (Eds.). Ethnicity and Aging, Theory, Research and Policy. New York: Springer Publishing Company, 32-65.

This chapter discusses the importance of ethnicity throughout American history in social provision for the aged. The underlying assumption is that past experience can clarify current research and policy. Historical evidence cited presents a picture of abuse by public welfare, especially in almshouses. To avoid degradation of their needy aged, non White-English-Protestant groups, i.e., Southern and Eastern Europeans, the Irish, as well as the Blacks and Asians, developed their own ethnic networks of assistance. Jews were especially motivated by a philosophy of "taking care of their own". This attitude to public welfare prevails even today among several ethnic groups. Implications of this historical research are that ethnic private and public provision for the aged can still play a significant role when these are combined with government supported programs and delivered within culturally accepted services.

282. Lavender, A. D. and Forsyth, J. M. (1976). The sociological study of minority groups as reflected by leading sociological journals. Who gets studied and who gets neglected? Ethnicity, 3-(4):388-398.

A total of 482 articles published in three leading American Sociological Journals that represent 165 years of publication were surveyed.   Over 70 percent of the articles dealt with blacks, while no more than 6 percent of the articles dealt with other groups. The neglect of these other groups is glaring. Of the Euro-Americans only four articles dealt with Italian-Americans, only three with Polish-Americans and only five with Scandinavian-Americans. The Irish-Americans had only one article published by the Journal of Social Forces in 52 years of publication. The author concludes that this is why so little is known about the non-black ethnic groups and about their relationships with each other and with the dominant groups in society. The need to redress this imbalance and suggestions for future research are explicated.

283. Lazerwitz, B. (1973). Religious identification and its ethnic correlates: A multivariate model. Social Forces, 52(2):204-220.

White Protestants and Jews in Chicago and their religious and ethnic identifications were studied. Dimensions included ran from childhood home religious background to religious education, behavior, activity in ethnic organizations, and to concern over the religious education of one's children. Various measures of ethnic and religious identification were noted for Jews and Protestants based on socioeconomic status and liberalness.

284. Levin, I. M. (1980). Statement of Irving M. Levin. In Civil Rights Issues of Euro-Americans in the United States: Opportunities and Challenges. Washington, D.C.: U.S. Government Printing Office, 1980, No. 629-842/6080, 2-13.

The statement is based on a historical review of Euro-Americans in the United States from the early waves of the great immigration to the late seventies and the social processes that led to the creation of this category of people. Economic needs of many white ethnic groups combined with unresolved problems of ethnic identity culminated in the Fordham Consultation of Ethnic Americans which surfaced the nature of the white diversity, while contributing to a sense of selfhood among these people. Issues discussed center on black-white relations, on the many meanings of cultural pluralism, on government policies, on injustice, and on the need to train human rights workers to recognize and to respect the ethnic factors in their work with people.

285. Markides, K. S. (1982). Ethnicity and aging: A comment. The Gerontologist, 11:467-470.

Holzberg's 1982 article in The Gerontologist (reviewed) drew a spirited response and a defense of minority focused research in aging. Ignorance of the ethnic factor or ethnicity is far from being complete, the author states, and, when it is done, it represents the interest of the researcher in minority status, rather than in the broader concept of ethnicity. There is a general agreement by both authors about the inadequacies of the aging literature with respect to ethnicity. Their differences are due largely to the rationale they employ in defense of their perspectives, including appropriate remedies for dealing with the problems cited. The lack of comparable interest in white European-origin ethnic elderly to that of Black, Hispanic, Native, or Asian/Pacific elderly is attributed by the author to society's assimilationist orientation and to its tendency to define all whites as having similar traits, problems, and aspirations. There is a conclusion that thus far neither ethnographic nor other methods of research have yielded much knowledge about how ethnic-cultural factors influence patterns of aging or the aging process.

286. Matulich, L. K. A cross-disciplinary study of the European immigrants of 1870 to 1925. Doctoral dissertation, The University of New Mexico, 1971. Dissertation Abstracts Interntional, 32:5236-A.

The question of how could the immigrants from Europe become
Americans kept social scientists and writers of the era busy for
many years. Two views of assimilation into American society are
presented in this study: 1) the static definition of Henry Pratt
Fairchild's, which argues that immigrants must lose all traces of
their foreign origin in order to become real Americans, and 2)
Jane Addams' belief, according to which the majority of immigrants
could only become Americans if both native and foreign-born will
grow toward each other into one culture. The author opts for the
latter view.

287. Nugent, F. Mc. The disengagement theory of aging and retirement applied to clergymen. Doctoral dissertation, The Catholic
University of America, 1976. Dissertation Abstracts International, 36(10-B):5358.

This study sought to test certain hypotheses and logical exten-
sions of the disengagement theory of aging. Subjects were 150
clergymen aged 65 to 75 years, both married clergy, unmarried
priests in a diocese, and unmarried priests members of a religious
community. Two subgroups were formed: those with a history of
pastoral ministries, and those who had been employed in educational and administrative positions. Clergymen were found to remain
engaged in their work beyond retirement age to a significantly
higher degree than men of other callings. Married clergy had
greater life satisfaction than the unmarried priests. Implications of these findings on favoring the disengagement or activity
theories of aging are discussed.

288. Simic, A. (1985). Ethnicity as a resource for the aged: An
anthropological perspective. Journal of Applied Gerontology, 4
(1): 65-71.

Ethnic affiliation provides a broad spectrum of social, cultural, psychological, and even economic resources to older people.
Many of these remain invisible to the casual observer. This essay
focuses on the nature of ethnicity in American culture and the
positive role it can play in the lives of the elderly. The work
of anthropologist Barbara Myerhoff on the life style of a group of
very old Eastern-European Jews, who had formed a small "shtetl"
(or Polish-Jewish village) in a California beach community, has
become a classic example of the positive functions of ethnicity.
Despite their poverty and exclusion from the mainstream of society these elderly Jews were able to maintain a sense of self-
worth and dignity by their common sense of cultural identity and
mutual assistance in times of crisis.

289. Sokolovsky, J. (1985). Ethnicity, culture and aging: Do
differences really make a difference? Journal of Applied Gerontology, 4(1):6-17.

Do ethnic cultural differences make a difference to the elderly? This paper draws upon some cross-cultural generalizations on aging which have relevance to understanding the ethnic aged in the United States. Overidealization of ethnic subcultures have made it a policy error to place too much emphasis on the ethnic family and informal supports as the savior of its elderly members. In long term care and in mental health care especially, unrealistic views of the strength of the informal social resources and of the ethnic community can have the most unfortunate effects on the well-being of the elderly. Gerontologist are urged not to become unwitting contributors to this destructive trend.

290. Trela, J. E. and Sokolovsky, J. H. (1979). Culture, ethnicity, and policy for the aged. In Gelfand, D. E. and Kutzik, A. J. (Eds.). Ethnicity and Aging, Theory, Research, and Policy, New York: Springer Publishing Company, 117-136.

Three separate dimensions are judged to be the salient elements of ethnicity: cultural distinctiveness, ethnic identity, and life chance. Objective and subjective aspects of these dimensions for a wide variety of ethnic groups are discussed in terms of their influence on social policy. The models available for policy makers present different conceptions about the nature and importance of the dimensions cited above. The melting pot, invidious pluralism, the ethnic revival, and ethnic compensation are presented, and supported by research, as models for consideration. Anthropological data document the impact of culture on perceptions of roles, prestige and social interaction. These in turn affect both physical and mental well-being of the aged.

291. Winner, I. P. (1977). The question of cultural point of view in determining the boundaries of ethnic units: Slovene villagers in the Cleveland, Ohio area. Papers in Slovene Studies, 73-82.

The boundaries of ethnic units are explored using Slovene villagers' settlement patterns as data. Two approaches are identified: one based on region in the old country (i. e. Inner Carniola), and the other on distinct regions or micro-regions in the United States. Both can be useful in identifying ethnic boundaries because there may be correspondence between them as immigrants from the same area tended to settle near each other.

292. Zola, I. K. (1979). Oh where, oh where has ethnicity gone? In Gelfand, D. E. and Kutzik, A. J. (Eds.). Ethnicity and Aging, Theory, Research and Policy, New York: Springer Publishing Company, 66-80.

This chapter is in the author's own words a reflective and admittedly speculative interpretation of the development of ethnic and cultural research in the field of health care. Cultural and

ethnic differences in regard to physical illness have long been
documented. Ethnics have been stigmatized and blamed for their
assumed differences from the compact majority. They were accused
of having customs that perpetuate their own physical ills. In-
dictment of the individual for social wrongs is an age old practice. The nature of the illness may change, but the blame remains
the same. Viewing disease as an individual problem results in
seeking individual solutions, rather than societal ones. Ethnic
research of health care practices suffers from many pitfalls:
from the one sided use of the concepts of culture and ethnicity;
emphasis on the negative aspects in medical compliance by ethnic
people, stereotyping the subjects, and "medicalizing the daily
lives of the patients." The need to continually reexamine the
basic assumptions under which research is conducted is emphasized.

Education and Training

293. Huttman, E. (1985). Social Services for the Elderly. New
York: Free Press.

   This all-inclusive and detailed guide presents social services
and programs designed to meet the needs of the elderly, including
those of European-Americans. After reviewing the aged and their
needs, the author goes on to analyze the range of services available, setting priorities, using the informal support systems of
kin and community, and specifying issues that affect services
utilization. Chapters devoted to social contacts, meals, transportation, housing, adult day care centers, long term care in the
community and in institutions, and income maintenance are included
in the book. Problems faced by minority elderly and the importance of focusing solutions on specific needs are highlighted and
supported by research.

294. Lipman, A. (1978).   Ethnic and minority group content for
courses in aging. In M. M. Seltzer, H. Sterns and T. Hickey
(Eds.). Gerontology in Higher Education: Perspectives and
Issues. Belmont: California. Wadsworth Publishing Company, 223-
227.

   Meaningful theoretical generalizations and workable policies and
programs for ethnic aged must avoid the error of homogeneity and
uniformity of experience for members of similar ethnic groups.
Subgroups of minority and racial aged population clusters need to
be clearly delineated and researched, and their differences with
the dominant group demonstrated. Maxims such as that the elderly
population is predominantly female must be refuted by citing relevant statistics for specific ethnic groups. For example, Japanese-
American elderly have higher percentages of females than males,
while the opposite is true for the Chinese-American elderly. The
former immigrated to the United States in families, and the latter
mainly as unaccompanied males. Life expectancy of Native-Ameri-
cans is much shorter than that of Mexican-Americans (44 vs. 57

years), while the average life expectancy for the total population of Americans is 72 years. It is important to include material about ethnic groups in the curriculum on aging to learn about the dynamics of adjustment of different ethnic groups to social conditions, and to generate programs for those currently not reached by services which were designed for the dominant majority.

295. Palmore, E. B. (Ed.) (1984). Handbook on the Aged in the United States. Westport, Connecticut: Greenwood Press.

This handbook is a comprehensive guide to the older population organized in four sections: demographic groups, religious groups, ethnic groups, and those having special concerns. Sections provide information on demographic, psychological, and socioeconomic characteristics, history, particular problems and advantages, resources and organizations serving each group, and research issues and reference. The chapter on Europeans focuses primarily on three ethnic groups differing in time of immigration and mode of settlement in the United States: Irish, Italian, and Polish Americans.

296. Thernstrom, S. P., Orlov, A., and Handlin, O. (Eds.) (1980). Harvard Encyclopedia of American Ethnic Groups. Cambridge, Massachusetts: Belknap Press of Harvard University Press.

This encyclopedia provides the first comprehensive and systematic review of the many people who comprise the great human mosaic of this country.
As a major work of scholarship on a scale never attempted before, it is the standard reference to which scholars turn when studying ethnicity in American society. Each ethnic group is described in detail along with its history, patterns of immigration and settlement, and present conditions. The twenty nine thematic essays that illuminate key aspects of ethnicity encompass subjects such as current policy issues of immigration, prejudice and discrimination, assimilation and pluralism, education, religion and literature. Many of the articles on less well-known groups are the product of intensive research and provide the first scholarly presentation in English. Cross references and brief identifications of unfamiliar terms and alternative groups names, along with eighty seven maps which show where different groups have originated aid the reader, while annotated bibliographies contain suggestions for further readings.

297. Watson, W. H. (1982). Aging and Social Behavior--an Introduction to Social Gerontology. Monterey, California: Wadsworth Health Sciences Division.

This is the only textbook in aging that treats Euro-American elderly as a separate entity in the population. Emphasis is placed on research pertaining to the variations found in aging behavior among ethnic groups. Social organization, intergenerational relations, care-taking, and attitudes toward older persons are discussed in a comprehensive way. The book presents a detailed overview of gerontology that may be useful to students and practitioners. Issues highlighted include the social structure that influences behavior, health and social welfare of the aged, and seldom discussed topics, such as substance abuse and suicide in old age. Practical implications of the studies cited are provided throughout the 23 chapters of this book. There are three useful appendixes as well; 1) a guide to the literature in social gerontology, 2) centers and institutes for the study of aging, and 3) professional, service, and advocate organizations for older persons.

298. **Civil Rights Issues of Euro-Americans in the United States:** **Opportunities and Challenges.** A Consultation Sponsored by the United States Commission on Civil Rights, Chicago, Illinois, December 3, 1979. Washington, D.C.: U.S. Government Printing Office, 1980, 629-843/6080. Stock No. 005-000-00197-8.

The pluralistic nature of American society, and the diversity of background of the multiracial, multifaith, multicultural, and multilingual people who inhabit the United States have led the Civil Rights Commission to recognize the Euro-ethnics as a distinct entity in the U.S. population. The terms "Euro-ethnic American" is an umbrella term identifying persons of central and Southern European backgrounds. This term can be useful and also misleading for these people are not a monolithic group. Consultations held by the Commission with the representatives of many ethnic groups and with scholars and ethnic leaders helped to identify major issues of concern to the Euro-ethnic communities. They also led to a number of program plans and activities by the Commission on behalf of these people.

Conferences

299. **Final Report the 1981 White House Conference on Aging.** Washington, D.C.: U.S. Government Publication (No Number given). Volume 1.

This report is built on the comments, findings, and recommendations that emerged from the 1981 White House Conference on Aging. The report is divided into five chapters addressing areas of major concern to the nation and its elderly citizens. The first chapter discusses the importance of preparing our economy for the growing elderly population. Chapter Two deals with issues of income in old age and concentrates on Social Security. Chapter Three discusses the medical care delivery system, including long-term care and disease prevention. Chapter Four presents the social benefits and services for the elderly, while chapter five discusses the research needs and the implications of research for the national policy. Each chapter contains a set of recommendations developed by the delegates to this conference.

The 1981 White House Conference on Aging, whose theme was The Aging Society: Challenge and Opportunity, enabled millions of elderly Americans to become aware of the issues facing them. The 42 Mini-Conferences held in various parts of the country provided a forum for direct participation in policy-making and helped to clarify the choices we must make in developing a national agenda for the aging. National goals in aging policy include the following: 1) to provide the elderly with the maximum opportunity to live independently, and 2) to provide economic, medical and social support to the elderly who really need help.

300. Guttmann, D. and Kromkowsky, J. (Eds.) (1981).   White House Conference on Aging.   Report of the Mini-Conference on Euro-American Elderly, November 10-12, 1980.   Baltimore, Maryland: U. S. Government Printing Office, 720-019/6928, MCR-10.

The two White House Mini-Conferences on Euro-American Elderly held in Baltimore, Maryland and in Cleveland, Ohio (November 10-12 and on December 4-6, 1980) constituted vehicles for enabling elderly Euro- Americans to participate in the mainstream of society. They brought together ethnic elderly and their representatives from many different communities with the government in a mutual effort of policy-making at the national level. Recommendations resulted from this historic meeting centered on the need for the government to recognize the Euro- American elderly as a distinct and as an identifiable group among the minority elderly population, which includes resources that can be effectively employed in planning programs and in policy-making. Barriers to services delivery and resource allocations were identifed and strategies to overcome them were noted by the participants.

301. National Conference on Euro-American Elderly (1985).   Washington, D. C., Center for the Study of Pre-Retirement and Aging. Catholic University of America, 1985, p. 78.

This report highlights the proceedings of this conference. Major presentations include a demographic profile of the Euro-American elderly and an analysis of the significance of language and cultural barriers. Ethnicity and aging, family supports, neighborhood institutions, and the role of government are discussed along with model demonstration programs and church/synagogue services to the aged. Future policy directions for improving the well-being of Euro-American elderly are presented.

302. Roseman, Y. and Rosen, G. (Eds.) (1984).   Jewish grandparenting and the intergenerational connection. Summary of Proceedings. The American Jewish Committee, Institute of Human Relations, New York.

This report documents a scholarly conference on the importance of Jewish grandparents as links to the past and as factors in the identity formation of their grandchildren. Increased longevity had made grandparenting a mass experience, rather than a privilege of the few. Presentations include topics such as the Jewish tradition and contemporary reality, in which there is a need to revive the respect and the recognition for the old in general, and for the grandparent in particular; strengthening the "vital connection," and looking upon the family as a source of strength and as a healthy basis for the bond between young and old, and programming for the intergenerational families. Recommendations on how to achieve these goals are elaborated.

303. The 1981 White House Conference on Aging. Chartbook on Aging in America. Washington, D. C.:   U.S. Government Printing Office, S/N 052-047-00029-3.

The 1981 White House Conference on Aging brought together over 2,000 delegates-representatives of the elderly in the United States – and leaders in the "aging enterprise." Over 600 resolutions were proposed and debated. These aimed at influencing the existing policies as well as at developing new programs and services for the rapidly growing aging population to ensure the continued well-being of the nation's elderly.

This Chart Book was prepared by the Administration on Aging to assist conference participants with their task. It contains pertinent information on the aged in this country as to size, makeup, functioning and social and economic conditions.

Manuals for Services Providers

304. Hayes, C. L., Guttmann, D., Ooms, T., and Mahon-Stetson (1986). The Euro-American Elderly in the United States. A Manual for Service Providers and Ethnic Leaders. Washington, D.C.:   The Catholic University of America Center for Aging.

This manual offers the readers information, program strategies, and service models to services providers working with the Euro-American elderly and with their families. The manual attempts to be practical, and "how-to-do" oriented. It identifies funding and staffing limitations, yet encourages the development of specific programs modeled after any of the ten projects listed in the following areas: outreach and referral, housing, advocacy, health and long-term care, nutrition, education, socialization, employment, recreation, and volunteer services. The seven sections of the manual contain information on the profile of the Euro-American elderly in the United States, barriers to serving them, their needs and use of services, the need for collaboration among religious, ethnic and public service institutions, the importance of the family and training of service providers.

305. President's Commission on Mental Health (1978). <u>Special Populations</u>. (Volume 3, Appendix). Washington, D.C.: U.S. Government Printing Office 276-135/6522. Stock No. 040-000-00392-4.

Among the first government publications that recognized Americans of European ethnic origin as a separate entity among the minorities, this report contains testimonies gathered across the country from national and neighborhood groups and from professionals who work with them. The uniqueness of these groups and their strengths that grow out of ethnic identity are described. Recommendations for mental health services delivery are presented. Among these are the need to maintain positive ethnic identity, to employ models of service delivery that are culturally relevant to the various ethnic groups, and to train professionals to study and to work with their own groups.

7
Bibliographies on
Euro-American Elderly

306. Frisch, C. F. and Setzer, R. G. (1982). Bibliography/Film-
ography: Ethnicity and Aging. Salt Lake City: University of
Utah, Gerontology Program.

This bibliography/filmography is arranged by subject and cross
referenced by ethnic group and geographic location. The table of
contents lists only the major subject areas, although the citations are gathered by subheading under each major category. There
is no index. While the majority of sources cited pertain to racial minorities, some works on Euro-American elderly are also included.

307. Metress, E. and Metress, S. (1983). The Euro-American elderly: An ethnic bibliography. Monticello, Illinois: Vance Bibliographies (Vance Bibliographies Public Administration Series, P-
1328).

This bibliography provides an alphabetical listing under general
references of Euro-American elderly. Citations are to books,
journal articles, dissertations and published reports. A total of
43 works are included in this bibliography about the Euro-American
elderly.

308. Murguia, E., Schultz, T. M., Markides, K. S., and Janson, P.
(1984). Ethnicity and Aging: A Bibliography. San Antonio, Texas:
Trinity University Press.

This bibliography contains 1,407 references, cited and organized
according to subheadings, with 44 of them relating to the Euro-
American elderly. Subjects covered in the listings of works for
this group include comparative studies of white ethnics Italian,
Jewish, Polish, and Slavic Americans, and religious minorities.

309. Pane, R. U. (1978).   Seventy years of American University
studies on the Italian-Americans: Bibliography of 251 doctoral
dissertations accepted from 1908 to 1977.   Italian Americana, 4
(2): 244-273.

The 251 doctoral dissertations cited offer a panorama of subjects which are significant to historians and to social scientists
for understanding the situation of Italian-Americans and their
contributions to American society.   These dissertations encompass
a period of seventy years, from the first decade of this century
to the late seventies, and document the changes in lifestyles and
attitudes that took place during those years.   The small amount of
studies dealing with the elderly in this ethnic group reflects the
lack of serious attention to their condition by former graduates
of doctoral programs in this country.

310. Pane, R. U. (1976).   Doctoral dissertations on the Italian-
American experience, 1921-1975.   International Migration Review,
10(3):395-401.

A review of doctoral dissertations completed in American universities during a period of 55 years reveals that only a small
proportion of these works were devoted to elderly Italian-Americans.   These are, however, useful for scholars interested in
studying the acculturation patterns of this ethnic group into the
mainstream of American society and for understanding the cultural
barriers that they had to overcome.

Appendix:
Related Journals

The journals listed below can help users of this bibliography to keep their readings current.

American Jewish Historical Quarterly
American Journal of Orthopsychiatry
American Quarterly
American Scholar

Balkan Studies

Centennial
Chronicle
Chronicles of Oklahoma

Ethnic Groups
Ethnicity
Explorations in Economic History

Family Coordinator, The

Georgia Historical Quarterly
Geriatric Psychiatry
Gerontologist, The

Health and Social Work
Historical Methods

International Journal of Aging and Human Development
International Migration Review
Italian Americana

Jewish Social Studies
Journal of American History
Journal of Applied Gerontology
Journal of Cross-Cultural Gerontology
Journal of Ethnic Studies
Journal of Gerontology

Journal of Geriatric Psychiatry
Journal of Illinois State Historical Society
Journal of Jewish Communal Service
Journal of Long Term Care Administration
Journal of Marriage and the Family
Journal of Negro Education
Journal of Nutrition for the Elderly
Journal of Politics
Journal of Psychology and Judaism
Journal of Religion and Aging
Journal of Social History
Journal of Social Issues
Journal of Urban History

Labor History

Mennonite Quarterly Review

New York Folklore
New York History

Ohio History
Oregon Historical Quarterly

Pacific Historian
Papers in Slovene Studies
Perspectives in American History
Physical and Occupational Therapy in Geriatrics
Polish American Studies
Polish Review
Present Tense

Radical History Review
Religious Education
Russian Review

Scandinavian Studies
Signs
Slovakia
Social Casework
Social Forces
Social Research
Social Service Review
Social Studies
Social Work
Social Work Papers
Social Work Research and Abstracts
Society
Southern California Quarterly
Swedish Pioneer

Ukrainian Quarterly

Author Index

Abramson, H. J., 102, 141
Adelson, G., 199
Alba, R. D., 9
Aliberti, J. M., 10
Allen, H. D., 112
Atkinson, M. P., 157
Averbach, J. S., 11

Babchuk, N., 178
Bankoff, E. A., 158
Banks, J. A., 268
Barton, H. A., 12, 21
Baskauskas, L., 13
Baum, M., 269
Baum, R. C., 269
Bechill, W., 97
Beeten, N., 1343
Beleda, S. E., 159
Beliajeff, A. S., 14
Bengtson, V. L., 270
Benkart, P. K., 15
Bennett, L. A., 16
Berger, G., 142
Berger, P. L., 143
Berman, R. U., 88, 160, 192
Berrol, S. C., 246
Biegel, D. E., 165, 200, 201, 271
Blouin, F. X., Jr., 202
Block, M., 161
Bodnar, J. E., 17, 18

Brody, E., 166
Buhle, M. J., 134
Burr, J. J., 207

Cacciola, E. J., 19
Cadigan, D. A., 239
Chase, G. A., 123
Caliandro, G. B., 121
Calwert, W. R., 266
Cantor, M. H., 247
Capozzola, B., 20
Carlsson, S., 21
Caroli, B. B., 22, 69, 139
Caselli, R., 23
Cerase, F. P., 24
Chrisman, N. J., 122
Cicirelli, V. G., 167
Cinel, D., 70
Cohen, C., 199
Cohler, B. J., 71, 248
Collier, C. M., 103
Constantakos, C. M., 26
Constantinou, S. T., 27
Cook, J. W., 272
Council of Jewish Federations, 25
Creedon, M. A., 107
Cryns, A. G., 152

Dashefsky, A., 273

Davis, S. G., 135
Dravich, R. B., 144
Driedger, L., 28

Ellis, A. W., 29

Fandetti, D., 168, 172, 249
Felton, B. J., 253
Final Report, 299
Finifter, A. W., 72
Fishman, J. A., 89
Flynn, J. A., 240
Forsyth, J. M., 282
Fortune, A. E., 228
Frank, B. B., 30
Frederick, J. T., 137
Friedman, H. H., 145
Frisch, C. F., 306

Galey, M. E., 215
Gallaway, L. E., 1
Gambino, R., 169
Gans, H., 146
Gay, G., 268
Geis, E., 160
Gelfand, D. E., 161, 168, 170, 171, 172, 173, 203, 249
Gelfand, J. R., 203
German, P. S., 123
Gerrity, P. L., 241
Gerson, L. L., 98
Getzel, G. S., 216, 260
Ginsberg, Y., 31
Giordano, J., 275
Gitelman, P. J., 261
Gleason, P., 147
Gordon, A., 64
Greeley, A. M., 127, 274
Greene, V., 136
Greenstone, J. D., 73
Guttmann, D., 74, 104, 148, 174, 193, 194, 208, 250, 262, 300, 304

Handlin, O., 296
Hanson, S. M., 175
Harel, Z., 204, 205, 217
Harel, B. B., 205
Harman, D. D., 90
Harrington, M., 149
Hasselmo, N., 92
Harris, P. B., 219
Hayes, C. L., 206, 207, 208, 275, 304
Heller, Z. I., 65
Heslin, J. A., 195
Hess, B. B., 176, 177
Heumann, L. F., 257
Hewitt, W. P., 32
Highman, J., 150
Hill, P. J., 128
Hollander, E. K., 138
Holzberg, C. S., 276, 277
Hooyman, N., 22
Hostetler, J. A., 33, 46
Howe, I., 75
Hoyt, D. R., 178
Huber, L. W., 251
Huberman, S., 2, 129, 179
Hunt, T. C., 263
Hunter, C., 90
Huttman, E., 293

Isaacs, H. R., 278

Jackman, J. C., 76
Jacobs, J., 151
Jacoby, S., 34
Janson, P., 308
Johnson, C. L., 35
Johnson, C. J., 105, 106
Johnson, E. S., 218, 242, 252, 264
Johnson, L. M., 265

Kahana, E., 253
Kalish, R. A., 77, 107, 108
Kaminsky, P., 199
Kanouse-Roberts, A. L., 162

Kastenbaum, R., 279
Katlin, F., 280
Katz, H., 78
Kessler-Harris, A., 79
Kessner, T., 139, 254
Khan, N. M., 201
King, S., 209
Kivett, V. R., 220
Klaczynska, B., 80
Kleban, M. H., 222
Kleinman, A., 122
Knox, A. B., 91
Kogut, A. B., 210
Korvetaris, G. A., 36
Krause, C. A., 211, 221, 255, 256
Kromkovsky, J., 300
Kulys, R., 180
Kutzik, A. J., 281

Landfors, A., 92
Lareau, L. S., 257
Lavender, A. D., 282
Lawton, M. P., 222
Lazerwitz, B., 284
Lee, C. F., 3
Leonard, H. B., 81
Levine, I. M., 275, 283
Lewin, R. G., 37
Lieberman, M. A., 248
Lindh, R. M., 109
Lipman, A., 181, 248
Loneaus, G., 38
Longino, C. F., 181
Lopata, H. Z., 182, 223
Lopreato, J., 110
Lowell-Troy, L. A., 140
Lucks, H. C., 224

Mahon-Stetson, P., 304
Markides, K. S., 285, 308
Markson, E. W., 226
Martin, J. H., 131, 137
Mathias, E. L., 38
Matulich, L. K., 286

McAdams, C. M., 40
McCaslin, R., 266
McCourt, K., 99, 225
Meier, L., 66
Metress, E., 307
Metress, S. P., 41, 307
Meyer, K. C., 82
Mintz, J. A., 42
Monk, A., 152
Moore, D. D., 243
Morawskia, E. T., 43
Mostwin, D., 44, 111, 258
Munro, S. B., 45
Murguia, E., 308

Naparstek, A. J., 201
National Conference, 301
Natow, A. B., 195
Nelson, H. M., 112
Neuhaus, R. J., 143
Newman, J. M., 196
Novak, M., 100, 113
Nugent, F. Mc., 287
Nur, F., 93
Nydegger, C. N., 183

Olsen, J., 162, 173
Ooms, T., 304
Orlov, A., 296
O'Rourke, W. D., 124
Owan, T. C., 227

Palmore, E. B., 295
Pane, R. U., 309, 31
Papanek, H., 153
Pargament, K. I., 212
Pavlak, T. J., 101
Peyser, H., 138
Pinsker, S., 114
Prager, E. H., 83, 87
Pratt, N. F., 154
President's Commission, 305

Ragucci, A. T., 125
Rathbone-McCuan, E. E., 228
Redekop, C., 46
Roberto, K. A., 229
Roche, J. P., 115
Root, L. S., 130
Rosen, G., 302
Rosenberg, M. L., 213
Rosenman, Y., 302
Rosenthal, C. J., 184
Rubin, B., 126
Rudinsky, A. J., 48
Ryan, J., 155

Saloutos, T., 49
Sandberg, N. C., 50
Sauer, W. J., 175
Schultz, T. M., 308
Scott, J. P., 229
Seifer, N., 84
Serow, W. J., 131, 137
Setzer, R. G., 306
Shanabruch, C. H., 116
Shanas, E., 197

Shandler, M. A., 259
Shapiro, S., 123
Shulik, R. N., 230
Shwayder-Hughes, M. L., 231
Siegel, M. K., 51
Siemaszko, M., 185
Silverberg, D., 132
Silverstein, N. M., 214, 267
Simic, A., 288
Simon, A. J., 52
Simos, B. G., 186
Simowski, M. J., 94
Singer, M., 222
Smith, D. S., 5
Smith, T. L., 117
Smolar, L., 67
Snyder, P., 232
Sokolovsky, J., 289, 290
Soldo, B. J., 176
Spar, M. A., 131, 137
Spillman, D. M., 68
Stachiw, M., 53
Steinitz, L. Y., 233
Stolarik, M. M., 54, 55
Stoltzfus, V., 56
Stout, H. S., 118

Streltzer, A., 163
Strombeck, R., 57
Susel, R. M., 58
Suziedelis, G., 234
Szekais, B., 235

Thernstrom, S. T., 296
Thomas, K., 164
Tobin, S. S., 180
Torgoff, S. T., 85
Trela, J. E., 290
Tropman, J. E., 130

Ueda, R., 86
U. S. Census, 6, 7
U. S. Civil Rights, 298

Vecoli, R. J., 59

Vignola, S. L., 119
Vinick, B. H., 187, 236
Virtanen, R., 95
Vollmer, M. H., 123

Warach, B., 188, 198
Waring, J. M., 177
Warner, M. E., 60
Watson, W. H., 297
Weed, P., 8
Weinberg, D. E., 61
Weiner, M., 189
Weiner, A. S., 88
Weiss, R., 120
Wertsman, V. R., 62
Wiley, T. G., 96
Winner, I. P., 63, 291
Wish, F., 237
Wister, A., 164
White House, 299, 303
Woehner, C. E., 190
Wright, B. 245
Wrobel, P., 156

Yans-McLaughlin, V., 79

Zeff, D., 191
Zola, I. K., 292
Zoot, V. A., 238

Subject Index

Note: References below are to entry, not page numbers.

Amish, 33
  and continuity, 56
Anabaptist, 28
Anthropological theory, 276, 277
  basic group identity, 278
  resource for the aged, 288
Assimilation, 116
  American identity, 147
  and pluralism, 141
  Loyalties, 149
Assistance to immigrants, 77
  and protection, 81
Attitudes to the aged, 168
  and care, 171
  changing patterns, 177
  family assistance, 172, 185
  kin relations, 185

Basque-Americans, 45
Beliefs, 122
  caring practices, 125
Bibliographies, 306
  doctoral dissertations, 309, 310
  ethnicity and aging, 308
  Euro-American, 307

Caretaking, 236
  self care, 241
  value of, 237

Communication, 192
Comparative studies, 244
  German and East European Jews, 259
  Irish, Italian and Polish, 248
  Italian and Polish, 249
  Italian, Jewish and Slavic, 255, 256
  Italians and Jews, 246
  Polish and Jewish, 253
  White ethnics, 250, 254, 258
  Whites, Blacks, and Hispanics, 247
Comprehensive services, 194
  frontiers of, 198
  in crisis, 216
  needs assessment, 257
  quality of care, 258
Conditions, 123
  and ethnography, 241
Conferences, 298
  Jewish grandparenting, 302
  Mini-Conferences, 300
  National, 301
  White House, 299, 303
Contacts, 160
  between Blacks and Jews, 162
  grandchildren and aged, 163
Croatian-Americans, 16
  in California and Nevada, 40
Czech-Americans, 32

Demography, 2
  ancestry of population, 6

ethnicity and language, 7
historical data, 5
Jewish population distribution, 4
older Euro-Americans, 3
Death, 64
fear of, 124
Jewish view, 65
Dietary laws, 68
Disengagement, 272
of clergy, 287
Dress, 240

Economic distress, 129
Jewish poor, 132
Educational activities, 192
and training, 275
studies, 282
Employment, 133
family status, 153
garment workers, 134, 135
labor force, 137
skilled and unskilled work, 139
steel workers, 136
volunteer work, 138
Environment, 232
Ethnicity, 184
and institutionalization, 226
influence on society, 190
mental health, 227
self-help, 245
Ethnic associations, 205
and charity societies, 210,
settlement houses, 211
Ethnic culture and religion, 102
"Americanization," 109, 112, 116
and religion, 103, 107, 110
cultural religion, 118
Hasidic view, 114
oral history, 104, 106
social factors in, 115, 121
Ethnic groups, 71
and expatriation, 72
East European Jews, 75
European immigrants, 79
German emigres, 76

historical perspectives, 74
Polish peasants, 73
Ethnic identity, 61
among working class whites, 155
and meaning, 108, 113
and the new ethnicity, 100
Jewish identity, 104, 154
Polish-American, 156
politcial behavior, 101
search for, 111
Ethnic traditions, 64
care for aged, 67
filial responsibility, 66, 180
food consumption, 68
in dying, 65
Jewish and Mormon, 173
role of family agency, 191

Family, 167
assistance, 172
changes in bonding, 177
housing, 182
husband and wife networks, 176
Italian-Americans, 169
kinship network, 175, 185
relationship to society, 190
remarriage, 187
Russian elderly, 170
support systems, 181, 184, 186, 260
ties of the aged, 183

German-Americans, 76
Greek-Americans, 25
basic dimensions, 27
emigration to America, 49
identity variations, 52
in Atlanta, 29
in the pizza business, 140
professionals, 36

Health care, 121
beliefs and practices, 122
disadvantaged populations, 123

generational continuity, 125
  role of community centers, 126
Hungarian-Americans, 15
  history in Cleveland, 61

Illiteracy, 90
Immigration, 73
  and naturalization, 86
  history of, 85
  Jewish, 75
Income, 127
  and economic distress, 129
  characteristics, 131
  levels of, 128
  sources, 130
Information, 204
  and delivery of services, 266
  public services, 267
Institutional care, 219
  and ethnic factors, 226
  day care, 237
  impact on aged, 231
  programs in, 238
  risk factors in, 235
  social support for the frail, 228
  supportive environments, 232
Intergenerational relations, 157
  and living arrangements, 164
  contacts, 160
  differences in patterns of, 159
  grandchildren's group, 163
  interaction, 162
  of aged parents, 158
Irish-Americans, 41
Italian-Americans, 9
  assistance to elderly, 19
  attitudes toward, 20
  dress of, 240
  economic achievements, 59
  expectations of, 24
  experience of, 23
  games of, 39
  generations, 169

growing up, 35
information sources, 22
migrants, 70
repatriation, 69
role expectations, 242

Jewish-Americans, 2
  achievements, 11
  assimilation of, 243
  attitudes toward Blacks, 31
  estimating population of, 4, 26
  immigrant women, 34, 37
  immigration from Eastern Europe, 75
  increase in elderly, 47
  mothers, 42
  Orthodox housewives, 30
  perspectives on aged, 67
  poverty, 129
  relocators to Israel, 83
  responsibility to parents, 66
  role of religion, 51, 65
  self-care among, 241

Language, 88
  learning, 91
  maintenance, 89, 93
  preservation, 92, 95
  problems, 94
  significance, 96
Leadership, 150
Leisure, 144
  activity interest, 193
Life events, 262
  satisfaction, 265
Lithuanian-Americans, 13

Manuals, 304, 305
Mediating structures, 143
Mennonite-Americans, 46
  and continuity, 60
Mental health, 201
    and slum environment, 222

and the frail elderly, 228
fraternal organizations, 215
friendship patterns, 229
help in crisis, 216
loneliness, 220
neighborhood based, 227
of ethnic women, 221
perceptions of divorce, 218
psychosocial effects, 233
quality of care, 217
spiritual development, 230
support for widows, 223, 224

Naturalization, 86
Neighborhood, 165
affiliation, 178
and care of aged, 171
living arrangements, 182
supportive services, 188, 200, 201
Nutrition, 195
religious practices in, 196

Old Believers, 14
Old Country, 87

Peasants, 73
Polish-Americans, 43
adjustments, 44
changing of, 50, 82
socialization of, 156
Problems, 270
cross-disciplinary studies, 286
in definitions of ethnicity, 274
in ethnic identity, 273
provision for aged, 281
study of ethnicity, 276, 282
Programming for the aged, 145
and peer groups, 146
in retirement communities, 151

Repatriation, 69
Italians, 70
Jews, 83
Resources, 206
collaboration for, 208
use of, 213, 214

Role of government, 207
Romanian-Americans, 62
Scandinavian-Americans, 12
Self, 261
and networks, 148
help, 142
voluntaristic intent, 152
Senior centers, 203
Serb-Americans, 16
Slavic-Americans, 17, 18
Slovak-Americans, 48
and education, 54
immigration of, 55
Slovene-Americans, 16
aspects of, 58
ethnicity of, 63
villagers, 291
Swedish-Americans, 21
and the 1970 census, 38
success of, 57
Status, 197
and loneliness, 220
in slum dwellers, 222
survivors of the Holocaust, 233
women, 234

Textbooks, 293
encyclopedia, 296
in gerontology, 294, 297
on the aged, 295
Theories, 268
ethnic diversity, 283
ethnicity, 279, 289, 290
identification, 284
minorities, 285
research, 292

Volunteers, 138
and long-term care, 199

Widowhood, 223
and outreach, 224
women, 225
Women, 99
intergenerational relations, 119
middle aged, 166
suburban, 264
support systems of, 181

About the Compiler

DAVID GUTTMANN, Associate Professor, is Dean of the School of Social Work at the University of Haifa in Israel, and former Chair of the MSW Program at the National Catholic School of Social Service, The Catholic University of America in Washington, D.C. He is coeditor, with C. Hayes and R. Kalish, of *European American Elderly: A Guide for Practice,* and translator, with M. Eisenberg, of *Meaningful Living: A Logotherapy Book* (by E. Lucas) and *Humanistic Psychosomatic Medicine: A Logotherapy Book* (by H. Takashima). He has published articles in the *Journal of Cross Cultural Gerontology,* the *International Forum for Logotherapy, Generations, Human Development,* the *Gerontologist,* and numerous other publications.